Changing Roles
for Men on Campus

Ronald J. May, *Editor*
University of Oregon

Murray Scher, *Editor*
Greeneville, Tennessee

NEW DIRECTIONS FOR STUDENT SERVICES

MARGARET J. BARR, *Editor-in-Chief*
Texas Christian University

M. LEE UPCRAFT, *Associate Editor*
Pennsylvania State University

Number 42, Summer 1988

Paperback sourcebooks in
The Jossey-Bass Higher Education Series

Jossey-Bass Inc., Publishers
San Francisco • London

Ronald J. May, Murray Scher (eds.).
Changing Roles for Men on Campus.
New Directions for Student Services, no. 42.
San Francisco: Jossey-Bass, 1988.

New Directions for Student Services
Margaret J. Barr, *Editor-in-Chief;* M. Lee Upcraft, *Associate Editor*

New Directions for Student Services is published quarterly
by Jossey-Bass Inc., Publishers (publication number USPS
449-070). Second-class postage paid at San Francisco, California, and at
additional mailing offices. POSTMASTER: Send address changes
to Jossey-Bass Inc., Publishers, 350 Sansome Street, San Francisco,
California 94104.

Editorial correspondence should be sent to the Editor-in-Chief,
Margaret J. Barr, Sadler Hall, Texas Christian University,
Fort Worth, Texas 76129.

Library of Congress Catalog Card Number LC 85-644751

International Standard Serial Number ISSN 0164-7970

International Standard Book Number ISBN 1-55542-927-0

Cover art by WILLI BAUM

Manufactured in the United States of America

Ordering Information

The paperback sourcebooks listed below are published quarterly and can be ordered either by subscription or single copy.

Subscriptions cost $48.00 per year for institutions, agencies, and libraries. Individuals can subscribe at the special rate of $36.00 per year *if payment is by personal check.* (Note that the full rate of $48.00 applies if payment is by institutional check, even if the subscription is designated for an individual.) Standing orders are accepted.

Single copies are available at $11.95 when payment accompanies order. (California, New Jersey, New York, and Washington, D.C., residents please include appropriate sales tax.) For billed orders, cost per copy is $11.95 plus postage and handling.

Substantial discounts are offered to organizations and individuals wishing to purchase bulk quantities of Jossey-Bass sourcebooks. Please inquire.

Please note that these prices are for the calendar year 1988 and are subject to change without notice. Also, some titles may be out of print and therefore not available for sale.

To ensure correct and prompt delivery, all orders must give either the *name of an individual* or an *official purchase order number.* Please submit your order as follows:

Subscriptions: specify series and year subscription is to begin.
Single Copies: specify sourcebook code (such as, SS1) and first two words of title.

Mail orders for United States and Possessions, Latin America, Canada, Japan, Australia, and New Zealand to:
    Jossey-Bass Inc., Publishers
    350 Sansome Street
    San Francisco, California 94104

Mail orders for all other parts of the world to:
    Jossey-Bass Limited
    28 Banner Street
    London EC1Y 8QE

New Directions for Student Services Series
Margaret J. Barr, *Editor-in-Chief;* M. Lee Upcraft, *Associate Editor*

Contents

Editors' Notes

Changes in men's and women's roles have been one of the most significant social phenomena of the seventies and eighties. Initially, men struggled with their defensiveness and confusion in reaction to the women's movement. Before long, however, men began to see more clearly the limits imposed on their own lives by traditional gender roles. The constraints surfaced in such areas as difficulties in relationships with women, distress experienced in work roles, truncated male friendships, and poor health habits.

As agents of change, student affairs professionals have been on the forefront of the men's movement. In 1978, the first men's program was offered at the American College Personnel Association (ACPA) convention in Los Angeles. The program led to the formation of the ACPA Standing Committee for Men. Later, the American Association for Counseling and Development also established a Committee on Men. These groups have been responsible for a proliferation of convention programs on men's issues in recent years. In addition, the *Counseling Psychologist* (Skovholt, Schauble, Gormally, and Davis, 1978) and the *Personnel and Guidance Journal* (Scher, 1981) were among the first professional journals to publish special issues on men's roles.

Since the publication of these special issues, efforts to understand and mediate the effects of sexism on men have grown considerably. The impact of the work of Carol Gilligan and other feminist scholars on college student development has been widely discussed. Program interventions on such topics as men's roles, acquaintance rape, and homophobia have been developed. Campus ecologists have challenged us to address the systemic influences of institutional sexism. And, perhaps most important, growing numbers of male student services professionals have begun to courageously speak of their loneliness and pain, to question their life-styles, and to reach out to others in new ways.

This sourcebook attempts to summarize, reflect, and enlarge upon these developments. Our purpose is to enable the reader to more fully understand men's struggles with their changing roles as well as to envision new possibilities for promoting healthy life-styles for men.

In Chapter One, Ronald J. May describes gender role strains for men, reexamines the developmental challenges facing college men, and explores the critical elements for promoting change. This chapter provides a conceptual foundation for the remaining chapters.

In Chapter Two, Murray Scher, Harry J. Canon, and Mark Alan Stevens observe the current status of male students on campuses today.

1

The challenges associated with gender are seen more clearly by reviewing the basic nature and interaction of male students and their student services professionals, campus environments, and social trends.

Chapter Three examines the variations of gender role strain experienced by specific subpopulations of college men. Gregg A. Eichenfield explores the additional influence of cultural values and social prejudice on these men and discusses the considerations for intervening with these groups in a supportive and affirming manner.

In Chapter Four, Fred Leafgren presents ideas for developing effective programs on men's issues. Leafgren addresses the assessment of the need for change, the choice of program topics and formats, and the design of marketing strategies.

In Chapter Five, Beverly Prosser-Gelwick and Kenneth F. Garni explore male students' patterns for seeking and using counseling services. They advocate counseling styles and approaches that reduce the threat and maximize the impact of the counseling process.

In Chapter Six, traditional male roles permeating the administration of student services are examined. Jon C. Dalton explores the impact of sexism on our work roles, supervisory and collegial relationships, organizational structures, and career tracks. Dalton advocates humanizing our work environments through recruitment, training, and professional networks.

Chapter Seven provides an annotated list of selected publications, media resources, and organizations. Although many additional sources are available, only particular items found to be most helpful are presented.

In Chapter Eight, the editors summarize the principal themes of these authors and the challenges for the future.

Ronald J. May
Murray Scher
Editors

References

Scher, M. (ed.). "Counseling Males." *Personnel and Guidance Journal* (currently titled *Journal for Counseling and Development*), 1981, *60*, (4) (special issue).
Skovholt, T., Schauble, P., Gormally, J., and Davis, R. (eds.). "Counseling Men." *Counseling Psychologist*, 1978, 7 (4) (special issue).

Ronald J. May is director of the University Counseling Center at the University of Oregon. He currently chairs the Standing Committee for Men of the American College Personnel Association. Over the past decade, he has worked with men's issues as an author, researcher, educator, and psychotherapist.

Murray Scher is in the independent practice of psychotherapy in Greeneville, Tennessee. A founder and former chair of the Standing Committee for Men of the American College Personnel Association, he has written on gender role issues for men.

Developmental theories need to be reviewed to better understand and ameliorate the effects of gender role strain on college men.

The Developmental Journey of the Male College Student

Ronald J. May

The evolution of gender identity is an integral part of every college student's development. Each student searches for a personal sense of manhood or womanhood that affirms one's worth and expresses one's values and needs. This sense of gender identity is sculpted by societal expectations and designed to fulfill social roles.

In the seventies, the women's movement radically altered perceptions of possibilities for women, often leaving men feeling confused and defensive about their reciprocal roles. However, the eighties have witnessed new beginnings in conceptions of masculinity (Solomon and Levy, 1982).

The implications of these societal changes for student development are enormous. We are challenged to question our theoretical understandings of male development, to communicate new possibilities to our male students, and to develop innovative, yet effective, programs and services that encourage male students to explore their gender role consciousness. This chapter will provide a foundation for meeting the following challenges: clarifying the nature of male role conflicts, reviewing developmental theories describing these struggles, and considering critical elements for promoting male development.

R. J. May and M. Scher (eds.). *Changing Roles for Men on Campus.*
New Directions for Student Services, no. 42. San Francisco: Jossey-Bass, Summer 1988.

5

Gender Role Strain

All cultures distinguish between masculinity and femininity, yet the two are not always considered to be incompatible (Boles and Tatro, 1982). The earliest personality theorists recognized the basis for androgyny. Freud (1970) maintained that all human beings were constitutionally bisexual. Jung (1953) described the animus and anima, male and female representations respectively, as universal archetypes stored in the collective unconscious and capable of expression in both men and women. Later, Maslow (1968) and Rogers (1961) expanded our view of the range of human potentialities. They believed that psychological health was promoted by an intrinsic self-actualizing tendency to express all aspects of our humanness and to integrate polarities into a sense of wholeness. Research suggests this integration occurs most often at midlife (Levinson, 1978; Vaillant, 1977) and, even then, only for a limited number of men (Farrell and Rosenberg, 1981).

What forces keep men from expressing and integrating their "femininity" until later in life, if ever at all? Narrow and rigid social expectations of what is masculine and feminine have systematically instilled males with what O'Neil (1981) terms a "fear of femininity." Young males are enculturated with a male mystique emphasizing strength, control, aggressiveness, self-reliance, and daring. A strong negative emotional reaction is instilled toward the expression of such feminine characteristics as being nurturing, cooperative, vulnerable, and emotional.

The continual incongruence between natural human strivings and perceived social demands results in *gender role strain,* which Garnets and Pleck (1979, p. 278) define as "a discrepancy between the real self and that part of the ideal self concept that is culturally associated with gender." The harmful consequences of gender role strain have been clearly described in the popular literature (Farrell, 1974; Fasteau, 1974; Goldberg, 1977; Pleck and Sawyer, 1974). O'Neil (1981, pp. 206–209) has summarized these limiting patterns as:

- Restrictive emotionality: being unable to express feelings openly, to give up emotional control, and to be emotionally vulnerable to self and others
- Socialized control, power, and competition: a need to dominate and succeed over others to validate one's masculinity
- Homophobia: fears of being perceived as feminine or homosexual and/or of one's own sexual or interpersonal attraction to other men, based upon negative myths and stereotypes of homosexual persons
- Restrictive sexual and affectionate behavior: sexual expressions characterized by performance expectations and dominance over another in contrast to mutuality, sensuality, and intimacy

- Obsession with achievement and success: persistent and disturbing preoccupations with work, accomplishments, and eminence
- Health care problems: failure to maintain positive health care through nutrition, exercise, relaxation, and stress management and to attend to physical and emotional signals of distress.

Gender role strain results from the failure of traditional male roles to meet the needs of a changing world. Male students need more androgynous role models to identify pathways for resolving gender role strain. However, many of their male faculty and staff are also unclear of their own changing masculinity. This lack of clearly defined role models serves to perpetuate gender role strain.

College males may attempt to cope with gender role strain in a variety of dysfunctional ways. Many students continue to prove their manhood through competitions, sexual conquests, and shaming manifestations of femininity in other males. Other students withdraw from their conflicts through alcohol and other drug use, avoiding intimate relationships, or becoming overly involved in their studies. Successfully intervening with the confusion, anxiety, and fear underlying gender role strain requires a review of our understandings of male development.

Early Development

Theoretical perspectives of gender role development have expanded considerably in recent years. Feminist scholars have cited male biases in traditional developmental theories and research (Gilligan, 1982; Keller, 1985). These authors offer alternative views of female development based upon life experiences of women. By adding a clearer perspective of female development, we are able to better view male development.

Gilligan (1982) describes different courses of gender identification, for boys to separate from their mothers and for girls to remain connected to their mothers, which leads to two differing, yet complementary, paths throughout the remainder of their development. Male development emphasizes separateness-independence: identification through roles and positions, individual achievements, a distinct and rational cognitive style, and ethics based upon principles of justice. Female development emphasizes attachment-connectedness: identification through personal relationships, cooperative achievements, a diffuse, intuitive cognitive style, and ethics based upon caring and compassion. Gilligan suggests both orientations are valid, yet each may be more useful in specific life situations. Although men and women emphasize their separateness and connectedness, respectively, early in the development of their lives, both orientations are possible for each gender to develop throughout the life span.

Chodorow (1978) describes the process of gender identity development based on the mother being the primary caregiver. During the first few years, infants develop a primary identification and attachment with the mother. During these years, the male child is able to freely feel vulnerable and dependent. However, the need to develop his maleness requires the male child to separate from his mother and to identify with his father, creating an upheaval in his internal emotional world. In contrast, the female child is able to maintain connectedness with her mother throughout childhood. To maintain nurturance and protection, the male child seeks a deeper attachment with his father, who may or may not be emotionally available. The deprivation the male child experiences from his mother creates an inner experience of abandonment and betrayal. Rubin (1983) hypothesizes that this repressed anger may be the source of male patriarchal contempt toward women.

To protect himself from the pain of this separation, the male child develops a set of defenses characterized by firm and fixed ego boundaries (Gilligan, 1982; Rubin, 1983). The psychological principle of reaction formation is used to deny feelings of dependency and vulnerability. When he later feels emotionally needy, he communicates, "I need no one." When he feels inadequate, he communicates, "I can do anything." Thus, the foundation of male character armor is formed. While these defenses may prove to be useful in some situations, their rigid use is profoundly limiting.

Several factors may lessen the emotional chaos and the need for rigid defenses during this separation process. First, the mother may withdraw more gradually, neither letting go too abruptly nor holding on too long. Second, the father can be emotionally available to continue to provide nurturance and to model appropriate expressions of vulnerability and dependence. Finally, both parents can communicate a balanced set of male role expectations.

The expansion of the father's role in psychological development has been one of the most exciting advances in development theory (Cath, Gurwitt, and Ross, 1982; Cottle, 1981; McKee and O'Brien, 1982; Yablonsky, 1982). Herzog (1982) coined the term *father hunger* to describe boys who have been deprived of their fathers through separation, divorce, or death. Merton (1986) and Osherson (1986) expanded the application of father hunger to the offspring of fathers who were physically present, but psychologically absent or inadequate. Merton describes this hunger as "a subconscious yearning for an ideal father that results in behavior ranging from self-pity to hypermasculinity and frustrated attempts to achieve intimacy" (p. 24).

I was initially struck with the importance of father issues while facilitating my first men's group. During our early sessions, I noted that the most emotionally intense moments always related to an experience with a father. Initially, the group avoided the painful feelings by quickly changing the topic. As the group coalesced, however, the men spoke more openly of desperate attempts to still seek their fathers' approval or to act out against their fathers' wishes. One man painfully described his father's refusal to accept his homosexuality. Others found themselves pursuing careers endorsed by their fathers, but that had little meaning for themselves. Still another realized a resentment toward his father motivated his use of drugs. All of these men eventually acknowledged their unmet yearnings for their fathers' attention and acceptance. Such acknowledgments enabled them to become more autonomous and accepting in their own life choices.

College Student Development

Psychosocial Development. Recent literature, particularly Gilligan's work, has been summarized and directly applied to college student development (Delworth and Seeman, 1984; Hotelling and Forrest, 1985). These analyses discuss gender role issues in the college student's development of identity and intimacy. They also address Gilligan's contention that while the two tasks tend to be fused for women, the development of identity tends to precede the development of intimacy for men. Thus, my review of male college student development shall begin with identity.

Chickering (1969) describes the precursory issues of identity development as developing competence, becoming autonomous, and managing emotions. The male student typically pursues these tasks within the confines of the traditional male role. He views competence through sexual conquests, athletic achievements, and external symbols of status and wealth. The harsh demands of residence hall, athletic team, or fraternity peers often painfully punish failure in these tasks. One star athlete found his athletic career terminated by an injury during his sophomore year. Withdrawn from his peers and unable to envision a future, he sunk into a deep depression complicated by alcohol abuse. His crisis led him one night to park his car on a set of railroad tracks and to wait for a train to end his life. Fortunately, crisis counseling and treatment for his alcoholism enabled him to redefine his image of being a competent male.

Becoming autonomous is often confused with an overemphasis on self-reliance. Expressions of mistakenness, loneliness, and need of support are criticized as being unmanly. Male bonding occurs in the course of activities, but deeper male friendships are often avoided. Frequently, a nonsexual friendship with a woman becomes a male student's first opportunity to explore his emotional vulnerability. Learning to be vulnerable with other men, however, marks an important passage in redefining his masculinity.

Exploring one's feelings and learning to express them appropriately is an essential, yet difficult, task for most men. Male students have generally been socialized to only express their anger and aggression. More tender and painful feelings remain locked up. One male student charged with a date rape sincerely reported, "I thought she was saying no in a moment of ecstasy." His emotional naiveté reflects both his inability to manage his own emotions as well as to attend to the distress of another human being. Only through criminal proceedings did he begin to question his behavior and acknowledge his own and his victim's feelings.

The startling incidence of acquaintance rape incidents on college campuses (Koss and Oros, 1982; Miller and Marshall, 1987) reflects the male student's struggle in accepting his sexuality. In addition to being abusive to women, Goldberg (1977) describes how expectations to be a "sexual machine" impose limitations on men's lives. Male students must learn to resist such pressures. Furthermore, young men need to learn to become aware of deep feelings that have been sexualized, to process these feelings within the context of their personal and relational needs, and to make choices about their sexual behavior that promote their own well-being as well as the well-being of others.

Sexually repressive attitudes further limit students' exploration of their sexuality. One young man admitted himself into a psychiatric unit during an uncontrollable anxiety attack. During a follow-up counseling session, he painfully disclosed that his crisis was precipitated by his first experience with masturbation. He realized his naiveté and felt less guilty upon learning that masturbation is a common practice among college males! In addition, homophobia prevents some students from exploring their homosexual feelings and experiences. These students need a tolerant, accepting environment to acknowledge such feelings and to explore their possible incorporation into their life-styles.

As college men proceed in developing their identity and sexuality, they become more open to encounter intimacy issues. The consolidation of a separate sense of self reduces the threat presented by a move toward greater connectedness and fusion. The first sexual experience of men is usually outside of a relationship, with sex being the primary goal (Sorenson, 1973). However, intimacy increases as sex becomes integrated as a growing and enhancing aspect of a relationship. Sharing feelings, once viewed as a sign of weakness, becomes an opportunity to be cared for, to affirm and nurture a partner, and to resolve emotional conflicts. Whereas commitment was once viewed solely as a loss of autonomy, the benefits of striving for mutual goals become more apparent. Although most men will only begin to resolve their intimacy issues during their college years, an increased ability to be emotionally intimate at this time is critical.

Cognitive Development. Gender role consciousness develops in conjunction with the student's capacity to conceptualize male roles. From Perry's (1970) scheme of cognitive development, the entering freshman is often viewed as a "dualist." Freshmen easily aspire to the apparent simplicity and correctness of the traditional male role: strong, tough, unemotional, and self-sufficient.

The dualist, however, is eventually confronted with greater complexity. One male student faced disciplinary proceedings for striking a fellow student over a conflict involving his girlfriend. He initially defended his actions as those of a man protecting the honor of his woman! He was confronted, however, with the other student's perception of the conflict, his inappropriate use of force, and his girlfriend's capacity to defend herself. These presentations of more ambiguous viewpoints lead the dualist into "multiplicity," in which a variety of views are held as equally valid. During this phase, different approaches to handling a situation are valued equally.

In Perry's next phase, "relativism," students' viewpoints are influenced by the context of the situation and by their own values, beliefs, and goals. The aggressive student might question whether his behavior is consistent with his views of expressing anger appropriately and the need to maintain relationships with fellow residents. As students mature toward a "commitment to relativism," these choices become consistent with their life-style choices.

In summary, male students' capacities to examine their masculinity are limited by their level of cognitive development. An awareness of their developmental status may help us understand their "immature" behavior. In addition, we must target our interventions at a level that challenges them, yet remains within their grasp.

Moral and Ethical Development. Kohlberg (1971) extends cognitive development theory into the domain of moral reasoning. He maintains that students respond to policies and regulations, ethical dilemmas, and disciplinary measures based on their level of moral development. Gilligan (1982) criticizes Kohlberg's interpretation of morality as having a male bias. Her own research suggests women make moral decisions based on an ethic of caring while men make these decisions based on an ethic of justice. Gilligan maintains that both perspectives espouse a certain truth and each may be applicable in particular situations.

College men indeed make moral judgments based on an objective and impersonal application of rules and principles. Since most of our social institutions reflect male-oriented values (Schaef, 1981), this orientation holds a certain survival value. Yet, college males must also learn to understand, appreciate, and, in some situations, adopt the personal and compassionate ethic of caring. In doing so, the views of women will be more understandable and useful to them. In addition, the ethic of caring holds its own survival value in the maintenance of quality relationships and one's own emotional health.

Adult Development

A review of men's issues in adulthood is important for at least two reasons. First, increasing numbers of adult males are enrolling in colleges and universities. Second, to effectively serve as mentors for male students, male faculty and staff also need to be actively involved in their own growth as changing men.

Several authors have studied the development of men in their adult years (Erikson, 1968; Gould, 1978; Levinson, 1978; Vaillant, 1977). Each theorist has used a stage model to address particular developmental tasks for the various periods of life. Levinson (1978) describes early adulthood (late twenties and early thirties) as a time to create a stable life structure composed of (1) a dream envisioning life's possibilities, (2) mentoring relationships providing guidance for actualizing the dream, (3) an occupation, and (4) love relationships, marriage, and family. Gould (1978) believes young adult men need to let go of the illusions that "following in their parent's ways will bring success in their adult lives" and that "life is simple and controllable." Vaillant speaks of career consolidation assisted by male mentors who serve as transitional father-figures. Although these theorists also stress the need for intimacy, Levinson notes that "close friendship with a man or woman is rarely experienced by American men" (p. 335).

As men near forty, these theorists address the now familiar "midlife crisis." Parental deaths, children leaving home, and a heightened awareness of one's own mortality prompt a grieving process in which men review their previous life choices and accomplishments. Vaillant terms this period "a second adolescence." One of his research subjects described this midlife crisis as: "One part of me wants power, prestige, recognition, success; the other part feels all of this is nonsense and chasing the wind" (p. 228). Levinson believes the successful resolution of this crisis depends upon a man's ability to integrate four polarities: young/old, destructive/creative, masculine/feminine, and attached/separated. Depending upon their satisfaction with previous life choices, many men choose at this point to become more invested in fathering, deepening their friendships and marriages, making career changes, and developing new leisure activities. As Jung (1953) initially theorized, the midlife transition witnesses greater expression of the anima and a more androgynous self.

Middle adulthood (late forties and fifties) offers opportunities for implementing a revised life structure. Generativity becomes important in expressing a broader concern for the young. The inability to make adjustments at midlife risks stagnation (Erikson, 1968).

Later life (sixties and beyond) allows men to become the "keepers of meaning" (Vaillant, 1977). Reflecting on generational changes can create an appreciation and concern for life itself. However, prior developmental failures may lead to rigidity, despair, and a fear of death (Erikson, 1968).

Promoting Male Development

Models of Change. Several models have been developed to describe the gender role consciousness of women (Downing and Roush, 1985; Palmer, 1979). These models are helpful for understanding the relationship dynamics between changing men and women. However, less attention has been given to conceptualizing the change process for men.

Carney, Taylor, and Stevens (1986) have done preliminary work in developing a model of sex role transitions that is relevant to both women and men. The model focuses on group settings, learning environments, and leader roles that optimally match the developmental level of group members.

The first stage of this model, "preawareness," finds both sexes having limited and specific social and career expectations. Women tolerate an "oppressed" role while men accept an "oppressor" role. Carney, Taylor, and Stevens (1986) suggest highly structured learning environments at this stage, with leaders offering more support than challenge. Large mixed-sex didactic groups are combined with smaller single-sex discussion groups.

The second stage, "awakening," finds attitudinal changes acknowledging the oppression of sexism. Although men see that sexism exists, their behavior changes are limited to specific, easily identified situations. The authors advocate less structure, with group leaders serving as discussion leaders. Didactic and experiential exercises are encouraged to help students personalize the impact of sexism in their own lives.

In the third stage, students experience a high level of emotional involvement in challenging traditional roles. Women feel anger toward the patriarchal system while men experience guilt toward their own sexist attitudes and behaviors. Since attempts to ally with women at this phase are often resisted, the men are apt to feel rejected. Open discussion formats in same-sex groups are used to facilitate the expression of personal feelings. While continuing to offer support, the degree of challenge and confrontation is increased.

The fourth stage emphasizes review, reflection, and integration. While integrating old and new values, women seek to rebuild their connections with men. Men are seen as being more supportive of the rights of women and men. In addition, men need to bond with other men in examining male roles. Same-sex and mixed-sex formats are combined to promote the integration of old and new value systems and same-sex bonding. At this point, referrals may be needed to help students become involved in counseling, support groups, and educational and political activities.

The final stage witnesses greater congruence and fluidity between knowledge, attitudes, and behavior. Choices are motivated by a conscious striving to actualize nonsexist values. Active commitments are made to continued personal development and social action in changing sexist social systems. The leader role becomes one of a peer-consultant and resource person.

The model given by Carney, Taylor, and Stevens (1986) offers promise in designing educational strategies for promoting sex role development, both within individual students and their male-female relationships. However, much further research is needed, particularly in conceptualizing the process of gender role consciousness for men.

Environmental Influences. The campus climate has been characterized in recent years as a bastion of sexism (Sandler and Hall, 1982, 1984). However, the student services profession has become increasingly attentive to the effect of such dysfunctional environmental conditions on student learning and development (Banning, 1978; Huebner, 1980). This campus ecology perspective is useful for envisioning modifications in campuses that promote male role redefinition.

Blocher (1978) maintains that effective learning environments include three subsystems: opportunity, support, and rewards. The opportunity subsystem offers role opportunities that challenge existing self-concepts and risk one's self-esteem and approval from significant others. Campuses can offer male students such opportunities as working in child-care centers, accepting dates from women, planning noncompetitive games, and working with female student leaders. Although these involvements lead the student to risk being viewed as effeminate or even homosexual by some, they also promote a sense of competence and control as a more androgynous man. It is important that the requirements for mastering these roles sufficiently challenge, but do not exceed, the students' capacities for change.

The support subsystem provides cognitive frameworks for conceptualizing change and relationship networks for emotionally supporting the vulnerable learner. Nontraditional male resident assistants, for instance, serve as excellent role models at a slightly advanced developmental level. Classroom lectures and educational programs on sex roles can illuminate pathways to change. The entire cadre of student and professional student services staff needs to be more sensitized to the vulnerability of changing male students. Formal and informal counseling contacts, support groups, and resource centers have been effective in this regard. In addition, male mentoring relationships are essential for male students to heal the wounds experienced with their fathers.

The rewards subsystem offers feedback and opportunities to make applications of new learnings. Although extrinsic rewards are helpful, the student must also be rewarded with inner feelings of pride and mastery. Student services staff must be able to help male students confronting traditional roles to process feelings of guilt, shame, and rejection associated with these risks. Placements in internships and career opportunities that value nontraditional males allow the male student to feel rewarded for his developmental struggles.

From another perspective, male students will never be able to fully confront the sexism in their lives until their campus community also confronts its own sexism. Staffing patterns, policies, and student activities that express sexist values must be confronted and changed. Sexist humor and abusive relationships cannot be tolerated. Male students need to see overt expressions of an active commitment toward building a campus climate that promotes equality and honors expressions of humanness.

Considerations for Change. While the theories and models described in this chapter may appear to describe steady, sequential steps toward growth, the actual change process is often confusing and chaotic. Students may cope with their chaos by remaining stagnant or even retreating into old roles. These pauses and regressions need to be respected as times of consolidating changes prior to venturing forth into new territory.

Although this chapter focuses on student development, as student service professionals we must also attend to our own struggles with our manhood or womanhood. Our credibility and effectiveness depends on our willingness to take the same risks we encourage our students to take. Perhaps the greatest strength of male professionals is to occasionally share our own uncertainty and vulnerability with our students.

Finally, most of the developmental concepts presented in this chapter are based upon the study of Caucasian, middle-class, American men. Cultural, racial, and socioeconomic differences have a significant impact on developmental choices and change processes. We must be aware of these differences in applying these concepts to international, minority, and disadvantaged students. Chapter Three highlights these differences for various special populations of men.

Summary

Changing gender roles are dramatically effecting the college experience of our male students. These young men are being encouraged to explore new roles that emphasize emotional sensitivity and expression, vulnerability, cooperation, and intimacy. Yet, most of them have been socialized by, and must still confront, life situations that systematically attempt to humiliate them for expressing these qualities. Some college men have navigated these difficult challenges and have grown to develop themselves more fully. However, many others have simply become confused, anxious, and depressed. Others have retreated into more rigid forms of sexist behavior to the point of being violent.

Student services professionals need to assist these students in understanding and working through these role conflicts. This chapter has summarized developmental theories that can assist in such efforts. Traditional theories of college student development have been applied to changing roles for men, and recent works on male development and gender differences have also been presented. However, our efforts to research and conceptualize male development within nonsexist paradigms must continue.

Similarly, we must further conceptualize the process of gender role consciousness and design intervention strategies that promote it. This chapter has provided several frameworks in these areas. The remaining chapters will explore this change process and intervention strategies in greater detail. While our primary focus may be on our interventions with students, we must remember that our success is also contingent upon our ability to serve as role models and to develop campus environments that not only tolerate but also actively promote equality, diversity, and change.

References

Banning, J. H. *Campus Ecology: A Perspective for Student Affairs.* Cincinnati, Ohio: National Association of Student Personnel Administrators, 1978.

Blocher, D. H. "Campus Learning Environments and the Ecology of Student Development." In J. H. Banning (ed.), *Campus Ecology: A Perspective for Student Affairs.* Cincinnati, Ohio: National Association of Student Personnel Administrators, 1978.

Boles, J., and Tatro, C. "Androgyny." In K. Solomon and N. B. Levy (eds.), *Men in Transition: Theory and Therapy.* New York: Plenum Press, 1982.

Carney, C., Taylor, K., and Stevens, M. "Sex Roles in Groups: A Developmental Approach." *Journal for Specialists in Group Work,* Nov. 1986, pp. 200–208.

Cath, S. H., Gurwitt, A. R., and Ross, J. M. *Father and Child: Developmental and Clinical Perspectives.* Boston: Little, Brown, 1982.

Chickering, A. W. *Education and Identity.* San Francisco: Jossey-Bass, 1969.

Chodorow, N. *The Reproduction of Mothering.* Berkeley: University of California Press, 1978.

Cottle, T. J. *Like Fathers, Like Sons: Portraits of Intimacy and Strain.* Norwood, N.J.: Ablex, 1981.

Delworth, U., and Seeman, D. "The Ethics of Care: Implications of Gilligan for the Student Services Profession." *Journal of College Student Personnel,* 1984, *25,* 489–492.

Downing, N. E., and Roush, K. L. "From Passive Acceptance to Active Commitment: A Model of Feminist Identity Development for Women." *Counseling Psychologist,* 1985, *13,* 695–709.

Erikson, E. *Identity, Youth, and Crisis.* New York: Norton, 1968.

Farrell, W. *The Liberated Man.* New York: Bantam Books, 1974.

Farrell, W., and Rosenberg, S. *Men at Midlife.* Boston: Auburn House, 1981.

Fasteau, M. F. *The Male Machine.* New York: McGraw-Hill, 1974.

Freud, S. *A General Introduction to Psychoanalysis.* New York: Pocket Books, 1970.

Garnets, L., and Pleck, J. H. "Sex Role Identity, Androgyny, and Sex Role Transcendence: A Sex Role Strain Analysis." *Psychology of Women Quarterly*, 1979, *3*, 270–283.

Gilligan, C. *In a Different Voice*. Cambridge, Mass.: Harvard University Press, 1982.

Goldberg, H. *The Hazards of Being Male*. New York: New American Library, 1977.

Gould, R. L. *Transformations: Growth and Change in Adult Life*. New York: Simon & Schuster, 1978.

Herzog, J. M. "On Father Hunger: The Father's Role in the Modulation of Aggressive Drive and Fantasy." In S. H. Cath, A. R. Gurwitt, and J. M. Ross (eds.), *Father and Child: Developmental and Clinical Perspectives*. Boston: Little, Brown, 1982.

Hotelling, K., and Forrest, L. "Gilligan's Theory of Sex-Role Development: A Perspective for Counseling." *Journal of Counseling and Development*, 1985, *64*, 183–186.

Huebner, L. A. "Interaction of Student and Campus." In U. Delworth, G. R. Hanson, and Associates (eds.), *Student Services: A Handbook for the Profession*. San Francisco: Jossey-Bass, 1980.

Jung, C. G. "Two Essays on Analytical Psychology." In *Collected Works*. Vol. 7. New York: Pantheon Press, 1953.

Keller, E. F. *Reflections on Gender and Science*. New Haven, Conn.: Yale University Press, 1985.

Kohlberg, L. "Stages of Moral Development." In C. M. Beck, B. S. Crittenden, and E. V. Cullivan (eds.), *Moral Education*. Toronto: University of Toronto Press, 1971.

Koss, M., and Oros, C. "Sexual Experience Survey: A Research Instrument Investigating Sexual Aggression and Victimization." *Journal of Consulting Psychology*, 1982, *50*, 455–457.

Levinson, D. J. *The Seasons of a Man's Life*. New York: Knopf, 1978.

McKee, L., and O'Brien, M. *The Father Figure*. New York: Tavistock, 1982.

Maslow, A. *Toward a Psychology of Being*. New York: Van Nostrand Reinhold, 1968.

Merton, A. "Father Hunger." *New Age Journal*, 1986, *94*, 22–29.

Miller, B., and Marshall, J. C. "Coercive Sex on the University Campus." *Journal of College Student Personnel*, 1987, *28*, 38–47.

O'Neil, J. M. "Patterns of Gender Role Conflict and Strain: Sexism and Fear of Femininity in Men's Lives." *Personnel and Guidance Journal*, 1981, *60*, 203–210.

Osherson, S. "Finding Our Fathers." *Utne Reader*, Apr./May 1986, pp. 36–39.

Palmer, J. A. "Stages of Women's Awareness: The Process of Consciousness Raising." *Social Change: Ideas and Applications*, 1979, *9*, 1–11.

Perry, W. *Forms of Intellectual and Ethical Development in the College Years: A Scheme*. New York: Holt, Rinehart & Winston, 1970.

Pleck, J. H., and Sawyer, J. *Men and Masculinity*. Englewood Cliffs, N.J.: Prentice Hall, 1974.

Rogers, C. R. *On Becoming a Person*. Boston: Houghton Mifflin, 1961.

Rubin, L. B. *Intimate Strangers*. New York: Harper & Row, 1983.

Sandler, B. R., and Hall, R. M. *The Classroom Climate: A Chilly One for Women?* Washington, D.C.: Association of American Colleges, 1982.

Sandler, B. R., and Hall, R. M. *Out of Classroom: A Chilly Climate for Women?* Washington, D.C.: Association of American Colleges, 1984.

Schaef, A. W. *Women's Reality*. Minneapolis, Minn.: Winston Press, 1981.

Solomon, K., and Levy, N. B. *Men in Transition: Theory and Therapy.* New York: Plenum Press, 1982.

Sorenson, R. C. *Adolescent Sexuality in Contemporary America.* New York: World Publishing, 1973.

Vaillant, G. E. *Adaptation to Life.* Boston: Little, Brown, 1977.

Yablonsky, L. *Fathers and Sons.* New York: Simon & Schuster, 1982.

Ronald J. May is director of the University Counseling Center at the University of Oregon. He currently chairs the Standing Committee for Men of the American College Personnel Association. Over the past decade, he has worked with men's issues as an author, researcher, educator, and psychotherapist.

Implications of changing gender roles are examined for the male student, student affairs professionals, and the college environment.

New Perspectives on Masculinity in the College Environment

Murray Scher, Harry J. Canon, Mark Alan Stevens

Within the last dozen years (Pleck and Sawyer, 1974; Fasteau, 1974; David and Brannon, 1976) attention has been focused on the impact of male gender roles on men and on our culture, including the attendant gender role strain and its effects, with a specific emphasis on the effect of gender roles on the university environment (Scher, Canon, Heppner, and Petz, 1982). This chapter will examine how male gender roles affect men involved in collegiate institutions and how those effects have an impact on the environment. The authors will examine characteristics of male college students, male student affairs professionals, and collegiate environments. The effects of gender role strain on students, student affairs professionals, and the collegiate environment as a whole will be explored. The remediation of the negative effects of male gender roles on collegiate environments will be considered.

What Are Male College Students Like?

Male college students are usually late adolescent males experiencing the developmental tasks of their age group. Although now they may

R. J. May and M. Scher (eds.). *Changing Roles for Men on Campus.*
New Directions for Student Services, no. 42. San Francisco: Jossey-Bass, Summer 1988.

be somewhat older males as the demographic characteristics of college students have shifted, many of the developmental tasks remain the same as issues of identity development and goal setting are a major preoccupation of men through their twenties and into their thirties regardless of other characteristics, such as race, class, and ethnicity. The gender role strains so important in understanding the behavior of older adult men are of less consequence in the conscious behavior of younger college men, although these gender role qualities are shaping the men they will become. Because colleges and universities are protected, often coddling, environments removed from many of the grim realities of ordinary life, many male students do not realize the consequences that the demands of their gender roles are having on their actions and thoughts. The strain is often present, but they are not yet willing or sometimes able to bring it to consciousness.

According to Chickering (Good and May, 1987), the central task for college students is the development of identity. Erikson (1950) also held this belief; he described this particular stage as conflict between identity and role confusion. It is quite clear to those working with college students that students struggle to achieve a sense of themselves. They struggle to acquire a corpus of beliefs and attitudes to define themselves in relation to the rest of the world, as well as to aid them in making sense out of the perceived world in which they must live. They come to the college environment with the cultural values they have inherited from their families and that they have been taught in school and church. Although older adult male college students have a stronger sense of self and a more congealed value system, they also are wrestling with new ideas and possibilities.

The second major task for younger college men is to learn how to develop, initiate, and maintain relationships with their chosen loved ones. The imperative to pair off spurs them on to continue and deepen relationships. The attempt to be mindful of cultural prescriptions and proscriptions, as well as the press of their physiology, causes many younger college men to experience anguish and compulsion in the drive to establish romantic relationships and to understand the intricacies of maintaining such interactions.

The third major task for younger college men is the separation from families. Most families cling rather tenaciously to their offspring. Colleges and universities provide a place to diminish and, in fact, end the powerful hold of the family. This is an important transition for all students but is especially significant for males as independence and autonomy are major elements of the male gender role.

The interaction of these developmental tasks—identity development, relationships acquisition, and separation from family—is further complicated by the achievement orientation of most males. There is a powerful push to accomplish all tasks successfully, and thus the driven quality of men emerges. The collegiate environment, with its seeming gentility quality and adherence to matters of the mind, confuses the developing man as it amplifies the strain he is under because it often does not provide real assistance in resolving his dilemmas. The competitive quality of the environment adds to his difficulty. This difficulty is further compounded by the contemporary value orientation of our society, which stresses achievement at any cost. The older college male is also confronted by the competitive quality of collegiate institutions and is required to face his own issues of fear of failure and need to achieve.

As eternal verities and long-standing ethical and moral absolutes rapidly decline, the college man is faced with a situationally and contextually determined values orientation. Our society has, at the same time, become more conservative, in regard to the pursuit of financial success and fame, and more profeminist as well as more accepting of the rights of minorities, both ethnic and sexual. Our culture has become more attuned to the physical environment, nuclear issues, wellness concerns, drug abuse, and health concerns. Add to this an increasing awareness of male gender role strains, and the contemporary male in a collegiate environment is beset with a tangle of issues, concerns, and labyrinthine passages to travel in his quest for his place in society while pursuing satisfaction in himself.

The result for most males is stress and strain as they try to wend their way toward equilibrium. Many men experience confusion and disorientation in college and universities as an outcome of the conflicting demands and expectations of the culture in which they have been socialized and the society to which they now aspire. The pushes and pulls are often extreme, and the strain can be enormous, with attendant dysfunctional behavior and much psychic pain. There is also a surprising lack of support for the difficulties these men experience. While education is often regarded as a female enterprise, colleges and universities are male institutions that value individuals making it on their own. Therefore, the ethos is not supportive of the student in distress but rather expects him to achieve what he needs without a great deal of assistance. This, of course, has been a traditional view and one always contradictory to the student affairs viewpoint, except where it too was victim to traditional masculine values. This traditional stance in regard to men has begun to change.

What Are Male Student Affairs Professionals Like?

Male student affairs professionals are, of course, like men in general. The great majority of men socialized in our culture share similar qualities of emotional restriction and presentation of self as strong, competitive, driven to achieve, and entitled to power (Scher, 1979). Males grow up acculturated to an ideal of individuality, self-reliance, and financial success. Therefore, to want to work in an academic environment is suspect. Homophobic attitudes, which are endemic to our culture, cause student affairs professionals to be in some conflict and, therefore, to emphasize the power and control possibilities in their work at the expense of the more feminine relational qualities that their work often requires and from which it could benefit. These men are often first-generation college students and are sufficiently enamored of collegiate environments to remain in that setting. It is their first glimpse of the promised life of knowledge and apparent gentility of which their less-educated forebears had dreamed.

Male student affairs professionals are unlike most men in that they are interested in education and in an occupation that does not promise great financial rewards. It is a profession that involves caring for and relating to people on a sometimes intimate and always personal level. It suggests nurturance and caring, qualities not seen as important to men in our society. In general, these men are "softer," choosing a career that, at least in its early stages, necessitates close, personal interaction with students. Although they are often attracted by this opportunity for involvement, which demonstrates some of their qualities and interests, later career tasks involve the more traditionally male pursuits of power, control, and domination. Men in student affairs are also choosing an environment that appears humane, although the collegiate environment is fraught with many of the same stressors that other work environments contain, in spite of its historical role as an ivory tower.

The fact that the environment is not as humane as new professionals assume is a cause for stress. There is competition, not only with men but also with women, who have always had a strong position in this profession and have in fact been drawn to it because it did provide a place where they could succeed. Aside from competition are all the other tasks that go into establishing and maintaining oneself in a work environment. Student affairs professionals have some particular problems in integrating into a new work environment (Scher and Barr, 1979). The naturally nurturant qualities of the men in this field are stymied by the demands of a professional environment that, like most professional environments, does not approve of the human qualities of nurturance, concern, and care (Scher, Canon, Heppner, and Petz, 1982).

It is hard to generalize, yet while housing directors, student activities directors, counselors, and vice-presidents for students affairs are not identical, as men they share qualities of striving for and expecting power, needing to be emotionally cautious, being strongly competitive, and pursuing success. These qualities may ensure success and achievement for some, but they also ensure frustration and disappointment for those who do not succeed. The tasks of student affairs professionals are difficult enough without the added burdens and complications of the expectations of the male gender role, whose strains are present for all men.

What Is the Collegiate Environment Like?

College and university campuses, in the second half of the eighties, feel somehow quite masculine. ROTC uniforms are once again ubiquitous; being competitive or otherwise asserting personal needs over those of others or society at large are again acceptable and possibly normative; being mentally and physically tough are "good things" to be; and pragmatism, as a value, relegates idealism to the status of a rarely afforded luxury.

It is likely that we are experiencing another swing of the pendulum, that we are once again momentarily at the hypermasculine end of the continuum, and that these symptoms of preoccupation and concern with "maleness" will eventually subside and be less dominant. It may also be instructive to examine briefly the nature of masculinity on the campus in its current incarnation.

The feminist struggle of the last twenty years has introduced lasting, possibly irreversible, change to the campus at all levels. Most significant, women are physically present in sex-integrated programs on college and university campuses in sufficient numbers to form a critical mass. Programs in business administration have dramatically increased the proportion of women students; professional schools (law and medicine in particular), which once deliberately excluded women, are enrolling women in virtually equal proportions to men; ROTC programs are enjoying popularity with increasing numbers of women students. The absolute physical presence of women in nearly every classroom and program has created a change not likely to be reversed, and male academic domains appear to have been permanently abolished.

The feminist movement, as an active agent of continuing social change on the campus, on the other hand, has slowed considerably. The younger generation of women students in the academic programs noted above views its fairly unrestricted access to the programs as a matter of course and even seems unaware of the price paid by a previous generation of women for that access. Indeed, were one to ask a gathering of college and university women to raise their hands if they considered themselves feminists, there would be a dismal response. For whatever reasons, even the term *feminist* has acquired the pejorative quality once encompassed by the earlier expression *women's liber*.

Indeed, as women have moved into the academic programs previously dominated by males, they appear to have adopted (uncritically?) the stereotypical masculine values and operating styles that were a part of those disciplines. Competition, being "hard-nosed," rationality, prag-matism, and associated masculine values have become almost as much a part of the repertoire of women enrolled in these programs as they had been for their male predecessors/counterparts. Similarly, the display of more traditionally feminine qualities, such as sensitivity to human feel-ings, the monitoring of relationships, nurturing, and responding affec-tively, are viewed as signs of weakness, if not outright incompetence. The unfortunate, paradoxical consequence of bringing women students into the full range of academic programs appears to be the extension of stereo-typical male values and behaviors to women, rather than the more desir-able outcome of increased tolerance of and support for androgyny for men and women. In short, it is becoming a tough, male world out there on campus.

Gender Role Strain on Campus

Effect on Students. Gender role strain significantly affects students and their relationships. We see an increasingly male-oriented institution emerging in higher education, with greater value placed on the tradi-tional male traits by both men and women anxious to get ahead and succeed by material standards. Male students, not yet wise enough to understand or accept the press of the feminism that promotes the softer side of human qualities and interactions, are victims of stereotypical views of women and male relationships to them. This often culminates in traditional relationships and in some rather ugly treatment of women. Three examples of how gender role strain has an impact on students are rape, homophobia, and career choice. Certainly there are many other examples, such as heterosexual relationships, family relationships, and academic achievement.

Rape. Date rape, also referred to as acquaintance rape, and gang rape are not uncommon on college and university campuses across the country. Although not new phenomena (Kirkpatrick and Kanin, 1957; Kanin, 1967, 1969), they are apparently more prevalent today than in the past and more prevalent than the general population expects. Researchers (Koss and Oros, 1982; Lott, Reilly, and Howard, 1982; Malamuth, Heim, and Feshback, 1980) have been investigating the prevalence of sexual violence and rape among college students, and the results are alarming. Over 30 percent of women reported experiencing physical force to engage in kissing or petting, while only 6 percent of men reported using force to kiss or pet. Over 25 percent of college women reported experiences of physical force or threats of force from men who wanted to have sexual intercourse. It is quite clear that nonconsenting sexual behavior is occur-ring on college and university campuses.

Rape on the campus is a product of alcohol abuse, gender role strain (both male and female), sexism, and lack of positive role models. College students (and the general population) maintain a limited view of what constitutes emotional, physical, and legal definitions of rape. Coupled with this are strong pressures and desires to be sexually active. Men have much of their self-esteem contingent upon heterosexual activity. Therefore, the development of age-appropriate sexual exploration and experimentation is confused with the pressure and expectations of needing to "score." Most college-age men are not aware of the price they pay by becoming involved in subtle and not-so-subtle, nonmutually consenting sexual behavior. Most college-age women know they are being violated, yet their own gender role strain issues and age-appropriate sexual desires often numb or distract their feelings of being violated.

Alcohol is commonly one of the contributing factors in gang rape and date rape. It tends to reduce one's ability to make rational moral judgments and to heighten the value and impact of group male bonding and thinking. In other words, an individual has a more difficult time differentiating right from wrong, and if a group member starts to question his (or the group's) behavior, the group would most likely attempt to strongly squelch such dissent.

Although rape is an extreme example of the effects of gender roles on males, it illustrates the potential of such role expectations for severe damage. Men are a product of their culture, a culture that devalues women and at the same time lauds masculine power and domination, creating an atmosphere where interpersonal violence is not unusual. Rape is an extreme example, but there are many other instances of sexist behavior on the part of students.

Homophobia. Homophobia contributes to gender role strain (O'Neil, 1982). A sense of power is a quality that most college men value and attempt to acquire and maintain. Generally speaking, males in our society are thought of as losing "power" if they are believed to have homosexual tendencies. Homosexual tendencies may also be translated into having female qualities that are perceived as less powerful than male qualities.

On the campus, homophobia gets played out in a variety of ways. College men engage in hypermasculine behaviors as a strong defense against being labeled as homosexuals. These behaviors include not backing down from a fight, physical and verbal aggression, excessive talking and bragging about sexual conquests, one-upmanship rituals, emotional restrictiveness, and self-control (no tears or vulnerability shown). Hypermasculine behaviors lead to male gender role strain.

The consequences of homophobia on college men are subtle and not easily disclosed. If asked how their lives are affected by their fears of being seen as a homosexual, most college men would answer it does not affect them at all. On the other hand, if asked why they will not refuse one more drink from a friend or back down from a fight, college men mention (along with other reasons) that they want to be seen as one of the boys and not some "sissy." Homophobia restricts the potential of many friendships. It is not unusual for male friends to become competitive with one another as a way to guard against further emotional bonding. Homophobia keeps college men competing with one another and oppresses directly the college men who are not heterosexually oriented.

Career Choice. College men are limited to their career choices by our culture's restricted sex role definitions. The impact of feminism has opened up career options for college women, yet nothing appears to have expanded the career options for men. What are the criteria by which college men choose a career? How does gender role strain influence that decision?

College males lose a broad range of career choices as they succumb to the expectations of their sex role. Searching for power, they are most attracted to careers and professions that will pay them well and offer them prestige. These success-oriented careers are viewed as a means of attracting women (if heterosexual) and becoming the all-important breadwinner of the family. Individual choice becomes lost in the search for success. It is not uncommon to hear male college graduates of all ages say they wished they had listened to their hearts when they made their career choices. The consequence is that many men feel trapped and unfulfilled in their work.

Dual-career families are currently more the rule than the exception. Still, college men usually select a career without thinking about how that career choice will influence a family and their satisfaction as a member of that family.

Sex role socialization must not carry all the blame as, historically, career choice options for women were dominated by the "realities" of child rearing. Feminism helped to unmask those myths and prejudices. Men are faced with a different set of realities and expectations when it comes to child rearing. Historically, men have not sought or been encouraged to be active participants in child rearing. If that reality changes, so must their attitudes about career choice. In other words, if college men knew that it was socially acceptable and expected that they be active in child rearing, the pressure and desire to be the "breadwinner" might be replaced by an acceptance of being the "breadmaker."

College and university students are both a product of and a force toward modifying the mass culture from which they emerge. Therefore, the paternal and demeaning treatment of women continues on the campus, although the struggles of women obviate some of the former strictures, such as curfews, dress codes, and gender-biased career guidance. However, the sexism that is embedded in contemporary society still surfaces in the collegiate environment.

Effect on Student Affairs. The "feminization" of student services professions—a direct function of the increasing proportions of women represented at all levels in student affairs agencies and divisions—has led to escalated levels of gender strain for men and women practitioners. Even though most senior student affairs positions (deans, vice president, vice-chancellor) on most campuses remain in male hands, women professionals appear to be gaining ground rapidly. Middle management positions are increasingly the domain of women. (In just fifteen years, the authors have seen the composition of those attending the Association of University and College Counseling Center Directors' meetings shift from the presence of a scant half-dozen women directors out of nearly 200 attendees to nearly a third of those present being women.) At a time when applicant pools for entry-level positions typically include more women than men, directors of graduate programs in student affairs report radically declining numbers of males among those who apply.

The presence of women in such numbers has had an undeniable impact on their male colleagues. Even though we characterized the campus scene earlier as being heavily masculine in character, males in student affairs professions have experienced a consistent press toward androgynous behaviors and the support of feminist concerns. It seems very probable that that press simply reinforces the already established inclination, well documented in career development literature, of male student affairs professionals toward androgyny.

With a professional socialization that strongly reinforces androgynous behaviors, males in student affairs can commonly find themselves "odd man out" when interacting with faculty colleagues, and even more out of step with the behavioral and value expectations of male administrators. More specifically, administrative operations on college and university campuses tend to be heavily influenced by, perhaps "driven" by, values of the private sector: competition, hard-headedness, toughness, rationality. Such a climate can be experienced as very punishing to males who value cooperative pursuit of goals, sensitivity to the welfare of others, a willingness to express one's own feelings, and similar values. While the extent to which the latter behaviors are valued and reinforced in student affairs professions is obvious to those who are practitioners, it creates dissonance between expected values and behaviors as practiced within the confines of agencies and divisions, and the expectations in the larger arena of the campus, producing substantial conflict when male practitioners are called on to ply their trade in that larger arena.

It seems probable that those most affected by gender role strain are the men and women practitioners who work at senior administrative levels. Their assignments take them into the arenas described earlier where traditional masculine values operate and the repertoire of expected behaviors has a more competitive, rational, and pragmatic bent. Male student affairs administrators suffer because "sensitive" behaviors are judged as being signs of weakness and possible incompetence (one has to be tough to get the job done). Women practitioners have to counter the expectations of their non–student affairs cohorts who have determined that they (being women) cannot understand finances, have to prove that they will be able "to stand the pressure," and then, having proved themselves, may be judged "unfeminine" if they have played the game too well.

If, in addition, either men or women student affairs administrators take very seriously their role as conscience of the campus community, there will be an added strain of significant proportions. Taking a position on moral and ethical issues and sustaining a focus on matters of human dignity and worth will frequently result in a face-off between resolutions viewed by some as being quite pragmatic (part of "real life") and solutions that student affairs professionals would view as being simply just or humane. A not uncommon outcome of adopting the role of campus conscience—even when that role is nonstrident and devoid of self-righteousness—is a kind of "there-you-go-again" syndrome. The male assuming that role is disempowered when others in the structure choose to label the behavior as being idiosyncratic to the particular person and therefore not worthy of serious consideration. That kind of disempowerment can be personally devastating to the practitioner and particularly destructive with respect to attempts to implement the values central to student affairs professionals.

All of this underscores the importance of developing and sustaining a community of support within the student affairs community. Both men and women practitioners at all the administrative levels will encounter more sexist and less androgynous expectations when operating outside their individual agencies and divisions. Continuing attention to and awareness of that added strain make it possible for them to be more caring toward each other, not automatically lapsing into nonsupportive behaviors because some passing need has not been met, or because some administrative outcome generates disappointment, or because a colleague has seemingly let them down. The large issue is one of sustaining a community of support for those who would build a more humane campus and world.

Remediation of Gender Role–Induced Strain

The general remediation of the effect of gender role strain is slow going, but something is happening in our society that bodes well for the future. There is a trifle more humanity or humaneness, almost a ground swell, coming from the populace. There have been changes in society as a whole. We are moving slowly toward a more responsible culture, examples being seat belt laws and widespread publicity campaigns against drunk driving. In other ways, however, we have not advanced, and have even retreated, an example being the return to sixty-five miles per hour speed limits—a typically male choice of speed over life.

It is now more acceptable, but far from desirable, not to be hyper-masculine. One reason for this change is that many women are not willing to accept the bullying and intimidation that men have used in the past to control women. The demands of minorities have also made inroads on the control of the white male majority, and without intending to reduce the constraints of the male role, the effect has to some extent been just that. The men's movement has had a slight effect, but one that will continue to grow, as it is made up of people who have a strong commitment and increasingly are in places where they can exert influence, such as colleges and universities.

Remediation will come from cultural change and change in laws. As more men see themselves as people with emotions and needs and not as success machines or objects, they will expect and demand more changes. Paternity leave, once unheard of and now present or available in numerous places, is a growing example of such change. The emphasis on wellness has had a tremendous impact on men, as they no longer see themselves as destined to work until they drop. Unfortunately, much of the fitness orientation smacks of old-time male competition, which is often antithetical to wellness. However, that too will likely change. As men and women become more aware of the deadly effect of traditional male values and behaviors, there will be a change in our society that will undermine and eventually reduce the strains of gender roles.

Remediation in Collegiate Environments. College men face problems in relationships, marriage, parenting, and careers as a result of gender role strains. Tools for dealing with these strains are available on university campuses. They include programming, consciousness raising, counseling, and consultation with all segments of the college and university to ensure that a perspective that will reduce the constraints and restraints of male gender roles is adopted and integrated into the ongoing life of the institution.

Because the collegiate environment is simply a subset of the general culture, changes in that general culture will be necessary before collegiate institutions can change completely. However, as that institution has traditionally been seen as leading changes in society, it is important that modification and abrogation of negative results of gender roles be implemented in collegiate environments. As pointed out, the women's movement has certainly induced a great deal of ferment and positive change on campuses. It is now important that raised consciousness among males continues the positive direction toward parity between the genders.

The change in consciousness regarding male roles on campuses must occur on all levels and in all segments of the institution—faculty, students, and administration. As each of these segments changes its awareness and attitude toward gender roles, there is reciprocal effect with the other segments and a modification in the constraints and restraints of gender roles. Gender composition of faculties, although different from twenty years ago, is not significantly different enough. Students, as described, still behave in sexist ways that promote and are a product of male gender role strain. Administrators—primarily student affairs administrators—have often been responsive to a change in consciousness.

Among the ways in which colleges and universities have dealt with changing the effects of the male role are responses to rape, men's centers, and cooperation with women's programs. How a collegiate community acknowledges and conceptualizes the causes of rape on its particular campus will most certainly influence the nature and extent of rape prevention programs. For example, a collegiate institution that primarily views rape as occurring because of poor safety conditions will provide money and personnel resources for increased campus lighting, escort services, emergency telephones, and self-defense classes. On the other hand, a campus community that primarily conceptualizes rape as a social and systemic problem will spend its resources providing rape prevention programs and services for rape survivors and perpetrators. Of course, many institutions will incorporate elements of both responses.

The male-oriented culture on college campuses must be confronted by systematic, supportive, and holistic programs that address issues of male sexuality, gender role strain, sexual harassment, dating patterns, male development, relationships with women, homophobia, male career options, competition, and aggression. Ideally, these programs are designed to change the broad range of behaviors and attitudes that contribute to campus culture.

Facilitating attitudinal and behavioral change is a multistepped process, adjusted according to the cognitive and emotional readiness of the audience. At the core of the (re)education process is an appreciation and understanding that most men contribute to the culture through their ignorance rather than intention and through their pain rather than fulfillment. Facilitating change is best accomplished through helping men sensitize themselves to the pain they inflict on themselves as well as others as they buy into the myths of masculinity. The sensitivity process begins with the examination of how one has accepted a restrictive definition of sex role options and progresses with an awareness of new options and an appreciation for differences (Stevens and Good, 1985).

In order to reduce resistance and encourage change, it is important to communicate and treat college and university men as not being evil by nature and as being in some pain as a consequence of a restricted sex role definition. Inducing guilt usually does not sustain or motivate positive change.

The coordination and support of programming for men is an important issue. Historically, this kind of programming for men has received relatively minimal financial and personnel support, resulting in several negative outcomes. Lack of funding gives the campus community the implicit message that programming for men as well as for rape and violence prevention is not a legitimate request or need. The reliance on continuing and sustaining programming efforts is usually in the hands of volunteers or low-paid student workers; the result is a high rate of burnout and staff turnover.

A strong commitment to outreach, advertising, networking, and consistency in planning efforts is needed to build and sustain campus-wide projects. This can only be accomplished if there are adequate finances, space, and personnel.

Outreach and programming for men is not an easy task. Because offices for women, ethnic minorities, and disabled students have been relatively successful in their outreach and programming efforts, the authors believe that a similar model of outreach and service provision for men is needed if a campus is serious about helping men (and women) live relaxed, peaceful, and healthier lives.

An office of men's services is a timely, viable idea. The vision for such a center includes a variety of programs and services that would address the issues of many college men, such as confusion of sex roles, difficulty with intimacy, contraception, AIDS, sexuality, violence, hyper-competitiveness, fear of war, alcohol abuse, incest, rape prevention, sexism, and racism. It would be most important for this type of service center to align itself politically and cooperatively with a campus women's center and other student programming offices.

Trends in the Profession

On Campuses. As befits a relatively recent addition to the higher education establishment, the student affairs enterprise has less of the baggage of tradition than does its academic counterpart and therefore has been able to play a more aggressive role in addressing needs for social change on the campus. Certainly the first modest efforts of the feminist movement were more warmly embraced by student affairs professionals than they were by academicians. In bondage to their roles as conservators of tradition, even sympathetic academics—including women academics—were hard-pressed to find homes for the initiatives, concerns, programs, or formal course structures for women's studies.

It seems only fair to note the fact of the male presence and a numerical male majority in divisions of student affairs during this era.

While it could hardly be suggested that these males at this point in time were aggressively promoting feminist causes, it seems fair to observe that they were less resistant to the arguments of their women colleagues than were their academic division counterparts and were capable, on numerous occasions, of offering active support to the cause. It is also fair to observe that women in student affairs careers were willing to exercise considerable patience in educating their male colleagues about feminist concerns. That educational process and the restraint with which it was undertaken ultimately served men and women student affairs professionals well. Significant gains were made for women within these professions, and the women were, in turn, supportive of the efforts of men colleagues as they asserted and explored their needs as men.

The current trend on many campuses as an outgrowth of the pro-feminist history of student affairs professionals has been the support of programs and innovations responsive to male needs and developmental concerns. This has been indicated in this chapter as well as in other chapters in this volume.

In Professional Organizations. Several professional associations played a significant role in the evolution of the women's movement and subsequently in validating the emerging efforts of men to address men's issues.

The American College Personnel Association (ACPA) accommodated and eventually actively supported one of the first task forces (ultimately a standing committee) on women's concerns. The solid strength of that subunit of ACPA, as early as the mid seventies, set the stage for the formation of the ACPA Men's Task Force; that task force is now the ACPA Standing Committee for Men. The presence of this standing committee is a demonstration of and an impetus toward further explorations of male concerns in the association and in collegiate institutions.

The National Association of Student Personnel Administrators (NASPA) has long focused on the professional needs of the senior ranks of student affairs administrators and the institutions they serve. It is in reality an organization of institutional memberships (with provision for "affiliate," nonvoting members), with only one person from each institution having a vote. Most commonly, that person has been the senior ranking student affairs administrator. Inevitably, then, NASPA has been predominantly male in character, reflecting the numerical dominance of males in vice-presidencies, deanships, and the like. Women making their presence felt in NASPA in more recent years are more frequently represented in elected leadership and, in general, have gained influence in rough proportion to their presence in student affairs administrative positions on the campus. This obviously reflects changes in awareness of gender role constraints and a willingness to undo them.

The American Association for Counseling and Development has

acknowledged the importance of examining male gender role strains by establishing a committee on men. This committee continues to creatively explore the problems and to originate programs to deal with the issues unearthed.

Despite some very positive accomplishments for men both on campus and in professional associations, it would be misleading to suggest that those accomplishments and the progress made have been comfortable (or even comforting) processes and outcomes. The struggle has often been painful and taxing. The level of difficulty, however, is not the issue; the inevitability of positive response to and change for remediation of male gender role strain is the crucial factor in the further humanizing of higher education.

Summary

The authors have attempted to portray the intricate and often powerful role that gender role plays in collegiate institutions. Through examining the strains inherent in male gender roles and their effect on students, student affairs professionals, and the total collegiate institution, a picture of masculinity in the college environment has been drawn. Although there are many negative results of gender role strains, there is good cause for optimism as our culture in general and the college and university environment in particular becomes more humane.

References

David, D. S., and Brannon, R. (eds.). *The Forty-Nine Percent Majority: The Male Sex Role.* Reading, Mass.: Addison-Wesley, 1976.

Erikson, E. *Childhood and Society.* New York: Norton, 1950.

Fasteau, M. F. *The Male Machine.* New York: McGraw-Hill, 1974.

Good, G., and May, R. "Developmental Issues, Environmental Influences, and the Nature of Therapy with College Men." In M. Scher, M. Stevens, G. Good, and G. Eichenfield (eds.), *The Handbook of Counseling and Psychotherapy with Men.* Newbury Park, Calif.: Sage, 1987.

Kanin, E. J. "Male Aggression in Dating-Courtship Relations." *American Journal of Sociology,* 1957, *63,* 197-204.

Kanin, E. J. "An Examination as a Response to Sexual Frustration." *Journal of Marriage and Family,* 1967, *29,* 428-433.

Kanin, E. J. "Selected Dyadic Aspects of Male Sexual Aggression." *Journal of Sex Research,* 1969, *5,* 12-28.

Kirkpatrick, C., and Kanin, E. J. "Male Sex Aggression on a University Campus." *American Sociological Review,* 1957, *122,* 52-58.

Koss, M. P., and Oros, C. J. "Sexual Experiences Survey: A Research Instrument Investigating Sexual Aggression and Victimization." *Journal of Counseling and Clinical Psychology,* 1982, *50,* 455-457.

Lott, B., Reilly, M. E., and Howard, D. R. "Sexual Harassment: A Campus Community Case Study." *Signs,* 1982, *8* (1), 296-319.

Malamuth, N., Heim, M., and Feshback, S. "Sexual Responsiveness of College Students to Rape Depictions: Inhibitory and Disinhibitory Effects." *Journal of Personality and Social Psychology,* 1980, *38,* 399–408.

O'Neil, J. "Gender Role Conflict and Strain in Men's Lives." In K. Solomon and N. Levy (eds.), *Men in Transition.* New York: Plenum, 1982.

Pleck, J. H., and Sawyer, J. *Men and Masculinity.* Englewood Cliffs, N.J.: Prentice-Hall, 1974.

Scher, M. "On Counseling Men." *Personnel and Guidance Journal,* 1979, *57,* 252–255.

Scher, M., and Barr, M. J. "Beyond Graduate School: Strategies for Survival." *Journal of College Student Personnel,* 1979, *20,* 529–533.

Scher, M., Canon, H. J., Heppner, P. P., and Petz, W. *Male Roles/Professional Roles.* Unpublished manuscript, 1982.

Stevens, M., and Good, G. "Sexual Justice Domain." In M. Stevens and R. Gebhart (eds.), *Rape Education for Men Curriculum Guide.* Columbus: Ohio State University, 1985.

Murray Scher is in the independent practice of psychotherapy in Greeneville, Tennessee. A founder and former chair of the Standing Committee for Men of the American College Personnel Association, he has written on gender role issues for men.

Harry J. Canon teaches courses in counseling and higher education at Northern Illinois University. He takes pride in having two grown sons who are gentle men.

Mark Alan Stevens is coordinator of training at the Student Counseling Center of the University of Southern California. He is former cochair of the National Organization for Changing Men.

Special groups of college men exhibit variations in gender role strain and require different intervention efforts.

Needs of Special Populations of Men

Gregg A. Eichenfield

There is, again, a growing concern on college and university campuses for the needs of "special populations." In the 1960s in response to the concerns and inequities found by our "minority" students, services, often designated "special student services" by administrators, were established for men and women on campus. Many of these programs exist today in some modified form. While many believed that the militancy of the 1960s had passed (especially regarding women's programs and services), the recent outbreak of blatant racism on the campuses of U.S. colleges and universities has renewed a call for more programs and services ("Is the Dream Over?", 1987). Hidden in this group of concerns are the needs of male students with a variety of backgrounds, cultures, and demands placed upon them. As has been described in earlier chapters, issues of gender role strain, the masculine mystique, and the fear of femininity affect all men on our campuses. I will describe some of the concerns of various subpopulations of men and the effect of these concerns on their college experience. The reader should be aware that this chapter will be an overview of these concerns; space limitations prohibit the lengthy discussion of any subpopulation. However, resources will be provided, when available, to direct the reader to more extensive information.

In an attempt to provide some consistency, each subpopulation

R. J. May and M. Scher (eds.). *Changing Roles for Men on Campus.*
New Directions for Student Services, no. 42. San Francisco: Jossey-Bass, Summer 1988.

discussed will be presented in a common framework. This framework will include a brief description of the population, the specific issues of the group and its unique needs, followed by a description of possible interventions. The populations included in this chapter are ethnic minority men, gay and bisexual men, international male students, male athletes, fraternity men, men in leadership roles, men in dual-career relationships, and adult male students. The reader is encouraged to think about these groups and other subpopulations of men that may be of concern on a particular campus and to consider possible effective, unique interventions for a particular institution.

Ethnic Minority Males

The concerns of minority students attending institutions of higher education have occupied a great deal of time and energy over the past twenty years. It is only very recently that the specific concerns of men in these minority groups have even been described. Our perceptions of male minority students tend to be biased by stereotypes of both the male gender and the minority group itself. Some of these stereotypes include the following: the black male student as being only interested in athletics, sex, and "getting by" (Davis, 1981; Lee, 1987); the Hispanic male student as the caricature of "machismo," which includes the sexual double standard, the "mañana" complex ("I'll do it tomorrow"), and an unwillingness to attempt his best (Lara-Cantu and Navarro-Arias, 1986; Valdez, Baron, and Ponce, 1987); and the Asian male, plagued by a stereotype of being the hardest working and smartest of all college students (Lee and Saul, 1987). Unfortunately, many of these students are often lumped together by race, with cultural differences being ignored. College campuses have seen a tremendous increase, for example, in students from Southeast Asia (Vietnamese, Laotian, Cambodian, Hmong, Thai), each with a different language, culture, and diet; and yet all of these students are simply called Asian. It is also evident that the group termed Hispanics now includes many citizens and permanent residents who have escaped from the armed conflicts of Central and South America.

The gender role strain issues of these male students are not only tied to how "traditional" male college students act but also to the unique issues brought out by the student's culture. It is important when working with ethnic minority males that the student services professional be aware of the cultural ramifications of the student's needs and of any interventions that will be attempted. With this subpopulation, as with all others that will be described in this chapter, effective interventions must really begin with the training of professional and support staff to recognize and appreciate existing differences among these male students.

Interventions with ethnic males must take into consideration the cultural roles and mores of the student, and often the approach must be deliberate, thoughtful, and progressing over time (Davis, 1981). Attempts to create an ethnic male consciousness-raising group, for example, combining all ethnic males, might be met by great resistance, since many ethnic males hold the same stereotypes about each other that the majority culture holds, and they might believe little would be learned from such a group. Interventions designed to help a particular group of ethnic males (such as Asian men) learn about the particular impact that traditional male roles have on them would be more effective. Such programming, sponsored by student services, allows those men who share these particular stereotypes to expose themselves in a relatively safe environment of their peers where issues can be brought up and addressed.

As with any program confronting male stereotypes and culture, these programs should have specific goals (for example, breaking down stereotypes of other ethnic males, male health risks, ethnic men who are violent, and so on). When the program is being conducted by majority staff, ethnic male role models must be found whenever possible, and their cooperation and support must be solicited. Several sessions may be more effective than one-shot formats, and members should be encouraged to continue the identification and awareness process outside the program. One method that has been successful involves a series of workshops about responsible sexuality for ethnic males. While the first sessions involves mostly issues around the mechanics of sex, birth control, and sexually transmitted diseases, the remaining sessions focus on relationships between men and women, which usually leads to issues of sex role stereotypes and provides an entry into a discussion of gender role strain and possible alternatives. Given adequate support, a series of sessions can be provided to ethnic males that confronts the roles of these men. When an institution does campus-wide programming on men's issues, it would be quite easy to include workshops for black, Asian, and Hispanic men during these times.

Gay and Bisexual Men

The growing concern over the spread of the AIDS virus (Fradkin, 1987) has most likely increased homophobia and the verbal and physical abuse of gay and bisexual men on campus. It may have overpowered all gains that have been achieved by campus gay communities in the last ten to fifteen years. In addition, the fear of AIDS has created tremendous concerns for gay and bisexual men about their own internalized homophobia (the fear and loathing of homosexuals about sexual orientation and homosexual life-styles from men who are themselves gay or bisexual) and how it is affecting their relationships and their lives (Malyon, 1981). These concerns continue to grow in spite of the significant changes being made in the gay and bisexual communities on campuses relating to sexual and affectionate relationships. It is not unusual to hear student services and mental health professionals indicate that all of the gay and bisexual men they work with are affected by the AIDS crisis and the resulting fear and impact on their lives (Harrison, 1987).

Depending on the geographic location of the campus and the atmosphere created and supported by students, staff, and faculty, gay and bisexual students have made significant gains, have remained at a virtual standstill, or have experienced a tremendous backlash on campus. The needs of gay and bisexual men can then be described, based on where they have been as well as where they are now. Again, campus-wide efforts to educate the entire campus community may be the most effective method of protecting gay and bisexual students, as well as conducting proactive programs. The AIDS crisis has provided a unique opportunity for student services professionals to work with gay and bisexual students in conjointly educating the campus about the needs and concerns of this subpopulation. However, many administrators fear the alliance between themselves and the gay and bisexual community, and they hesitate to take action. While students and staff may not support homosexuality, the reality of the health crisis demands that we respond in spite of our biases and fears.

The needs of the gay or bisexual male student continue to involve such basic concerns as recognition, permission to receive financial support, and, at times, protection. In addition, gay and bisexual men are also very concerned about such issues as long-lasting relationships, responsible sexual behavior, career development, and sexual orientation, as well as the constricted behaviors promoted by traditional male roles and gender role strain. These issues can be addressed, but not without particular attention to the serious concern about confidentiality and privacy.

Gay and bisexual students are seriously concerned about their need to protect their identity in order to avoid verbal and physical abuse. For some gay and bisexual students on some campuses, these concerns are moot as they feel comfortable both with their identity and others' knowledge of their sexual orientation (they have "come out"). But for many students on many campuses, sharing that information is a very private concern (Coleman, 1981). Programming for gay and bisexual students should keep this issue in mind, and student services professionals should note that simply because they work in conjunction with gay student organizations may not be sufficient for some students to warrant attending programs.

Successful interventions with these students have included support groups, counseling groups, social programming (such as dances and other socials), and educational programs about health concerns, relationships, and programs targeted specifically for the gay or bisexual male to address gender role strain issues and how it affects them. Finally, student services professionals should be aware of the concerns that gay and bisexual students have regarding career decisions, especially as these students begin the job search process. Identifying environments that will be supportive of their life-style, whether or not to "come out" to employers and colleagues, and concerns about mandatory drug and AIDS testing are only a few of the issues that will certainly affect these students as they enter the "real world."

International Males

Over the past decade, there has been a growing concern on U.S. campuses with international students and, more recently, with male international students (Dadfar and Friedlander, 1982; Leong and Sedlacek, 1985; Manese, Sedlacek, and Leong, 1985). The plight of the international student, removed from his or her home, culture, foods, and entertainment has been ably described and addressed by such organizations as the National Association of Foreign Student Advisors (NAFSA). This "young man" (some are not so young) not only has to deal with the difficult language of English but also the stereotypes that Americans hold about him, the stereotypes he holds about American men and women, and the growing concerns of gender role strain and conflict. It might be amusing to view the miniscule number of international male students who even know what the terms *gender role strain* and *conflict* mean, and yet these students struggle daily with how they, as male students in a strange country, relate to American men and women. Again, the issue of stereotypes occurs, as international men from Latin countries are viewed as "macho," men from France and Italy are romantic, and men from the Middle East and Africa as viewing women as second-class citizens ("property"). Some of these stereotypes are maintained by these men themselves; female advisers of international students describe international men continuing to seek a male authority figure to give them what they want, disregarding the fact that the woman may be the ultimate authority in that office.

The needs of international males span all the possible cultural and racial configurations, but a set of common themes does occur. Such men are in need of education not only about American customs and mores but also in regard to their beliefs (often reinforced by U.S. films seen abroad) about how American men behave, especially with women. Many international men, especially older students returning to school for advanced degrees, begin their U.S. education by bringing their wives and children with them. They are faced not only with the pressures to perform academically but also with the severe pressure to provide for their family on a (graduate) student's stipend (although some of them are financially stable, either due to family wealth or state sponsorship). The loss of the provider role for these men, even acknowledging the relatively short duration of their time in this position, is often devastating to their self-esteem and may in fact affect their academic performance. The issue of culturally acceptable behaviors is of great concern to student services personnel, especially with those men who live in married student housing. Family violence is often discussed by counseling and international services staff as the most disturbing behavior exhibited by international males. While it is clear that most international men are not beset by these problems, those who are violent disturb not only staff but surrounding residents as well (Perkins, Perkins, Guglielmino, and Reiff, 1977; Anderson and Myer, 1985).

Interventions for international males are generally designed to increase their awareness of American culture beyond the stereotypes and to help them adjust to their new environments and learn to provide for themselves and their families. Again interventions conducted with particular groups of male students may prove to be the most effective. Students might be grouped according to countries, geographic location (Pacific Islanders), religious affiliation (Moslem students), or particular topics ("Dating American Women"), with interventions provided. I have found success also by inserting some carefully chosen international men in mixed counseling and/or support groups along with American students (the key for success here is the student's fluency in English—idioms as well as standard speech).

Humor has been found to be an important component to programming, as international men are generally more willing to relax and participate when their American group leaders are able to laugh at themselves. The issue of humor is especially important in being able to raise the issues of stereotypes and how these men believe they are supposed to act. It should also be noted, with caution, that many topics such as sex, birth control, nudity, and exposure (for example, bathing suits) result in extreme discomfort for many international males, especially when they are sharing these experiences.

The key to successful programming then is a sense of humor, a relaxed style of presentation, and deciding carefully on the combination of members in a group. International males are, for the most part, very interested in learning more about U.S. men and their culture, as well as willing to examine the stereotypes and their impact on our own culture.

Male Athletes

For many student services professionals, the image of the male athlete includes the stereotype of the "dumb jock," pampered by his coaches, given the benefit of the doubt too many times, not really interested in obtaining an education (Blann, 1985; Gressard and Sowa, 1983; Henderson and Weber, 1985; Wittmer, Bostic, Phillips, and Waters, 1981). Who more, given this stereotype, could be described as suffering from the impact of the male mystique, gender role strain, and conflict? Perhaps the greatest fear of a coach is to have the "competitive edge" removed from one of his athletes as a result of some kind of intervention on the part of student services. Perhaps that is why athletes are often so insulated from the rest of the campus and students, and the only time seen or heard from is when they are involved in incidents in housing (if they are not separated by "athletic housing" residences) or in campus disciplinary processes. The results of male athletes being insulated from other students, treated as different from their peers, and provided few opportunities to interact with other students (outside of the classroom) may result, for some men, in arrested development—not only in the area of gender roles but in all facets of their lives. This developmental lag may partially explain student services professionals being frustrated by the apparent immaturity of student-athletes (Harrison, 1981).

The needs of these young men are great. Many male athletes are minorities (for example, black) and have the needs of minority men described above, attenuated by the hypermasculine demands placed on them by coaches, fellow athletes, lovers, and their admiring (and, at times, degrading) public. It is evident that most institutions of higher education have love/hate relationships with intercollegiate athletics, and our male athletes must often bear the brunt of this ambivalence. Add to the above concerns the need to be a student and maintain a satisfactory grade point average (opinions are varied as to whether the NCAA's recent "Proposition 48"—the raising of academic standards and preparation for college-level work—will have the desired positive effect), and what is found is an extremely pressured young man, often asked to work the equivalent of two full-time jobs, study after practice, maintain his composure in the spotlight, and perform on the field (NCAA, 1987).

Many male athletes have been viewed as the hypermasculine image of the civilized warrior for years prior to entering higher education. As the selection process begins at younger ages (junior high school for many basketball and football players), such students are found to be accustomed to special attention, extra privileges, and the benefit of the doubt in various situations. For some, coming to college is simply an extension of what they have already learned to expect from others as a result of their athletic abilities and/or hard work on the practice field (Lee, 1983). And yet many of them are scared and immature, have not learned about the natural consequences of their behavior, and are inadequately prepared for college-level work and the pressures placed on them.

Interventions for male athletes are based on one critical component—access. As stated above, student athletes are protected from outside forces that might affect their performance, and student services personnel might never see athletes on their campuses on a routine basis. Beyond individual intervention in housing and through the disciplinary process, rarely will male athletes have the opportunity to be exposed to information that will describe and challenge their beliefs and myths about being male, and confront the costs of gender role strain and conflict (Hirt, Hoffman, and Sedlacek, 1983). Because of the perceived need to insulate athletes, intervention avenues may be few (Greer and Moore, 1986). A number of institutions have had success in meeting male athletes through required orientation seminars, required orientation classes (the University of South Carolina), and learning/study skills courses (the University of Utah). Some of the courses are required by the coaches who proactively try to assist the student in bettering his academic skills (Bausch-Altman and Whitner, 1986). However, most of these methods never address gender role issues and, unfortunately, when these students are seen, it is usually for discipline, academic difficulties, personal counseling, and, more recently, about the results of drug-testing programs (Gunnison, 1985). A useful resource for working with student athletes is Henderson and Weber's *College Survival Skills for Student-Athletes* (1985).

One avenue that has been successful in developing contact with male athletes has been those people involved in athletic programs who know the athletes and their concerns—trainers. These individuals, both male and female (and both professional and student trainers), generally know as much if not more about the athlete's personal well-being than many coaches, and building relationships with them does provide student services staff with a chance to be available to the athlete when referrals might be needed.

It should be noted by the reader that male athletes may be the most difficult subpopulation to influence effectively, and that the reality exists that student services professionals might be extremely frustrated in trying to gain access to a perceived "sacred cow" (Greer and Moore, 1986; Harrison, 1981). The campus community's commitment to athletics will play a major role in programs for these students. Generally, the larger the campus, the larger and more prestigious the athletic programs, the more difficulty will exist in obtaining access to male athletes and therefore addressing these issues.

Fraternity Men

Some student services personnel view fraternity men as the future of our country: the local, state, and federal leaders of tomorrow. To others, fraternities and their members are simply one more example of the "good ole boy network," maintaining institutional sexism (and, at times, racism) on our campuses. The stereotypes of fraternities conducting panty raids on sorority houses and "contributing to the delinquency of minors" through beer bashes and wild outdoor parties often overshadow the community service and philanthropic endeavors that these social organizations provide. And yet the image of fraternity men does in fact provide a caricature of men caught in midstride in maintaining the masculine myth, unaware of how gender role strain is affecting their lives (Orlofsky, 1978; Hirt, Hoffman, and Sedlacek, 1983). Such activities as "little sister" programs and rituals as hazing also contribute to the gender role expectations of fraternity men.

The needs of fraternity men include education and increased awareness about the challenges confronting "changing men" in our society, a serious and thoughtful look at sexism and the maintaining of stereotypes about men and women and the relationships between the sexes, homophobia, and male health risks. Fraternity men, and their female counterparts, in some ways epitomize the joy and freedom that most people think of when they view the "Greek" systems on campus: academic work, social affiliation, dating, parties, and the development of lifelong friendships. And yet they often are encouraged to view women as sexual objects, to match the stereotype of the "hard-drinking" fraternity man, to pull pranks and actually behave in the manner caricatured in the film *Animal House.*

Access, again, is a critical issue to student services professionals attempting to help educate fraternity men about the issues and concerns of changing men. Interventions generally have been of the large-group nature, where programming is provided on general concerns, such as responsible alcohol use, health risks to men, sexually transmitted diseases, and university policies and regulations. Other successful programs have dealt with such topics as AIDS and responsible sexuality, acquaintance ("date") rape, and career decision making, which includes discussions of gender role strain as it relates to work and career concerns. The issue of acquaintance rape warrants further comment.

When encouraged by their female friends or by incidents reported on campus, seminars on "date rape" provide a powerful way to both enter the male Greek system and have an impact on a community of men. Since acquaintance rape raises issues of power, control, dominance, sexism, and sex role stereotypes (for example, "Does a woman really mean yes when she says no?"), this topic allows men to discuss their beliefs about women and about themselves. The challenge to student services professionals is to share this information and encourage discussion with a group of men that might be resistant to the material presented.

Fraternity men often are the sons of traditional men who live in traditional relationships, and to challenge that belief system is not only difficult for the students themselves but also may raise questions about mothers and brothers and sisters and their role in the family as well as in society; some fraternity men describe feelings overwhelmed by so many concerns at once (Dickerson and Hester, 1982). They are capable of making changes in their lives and can be assisted simply by the knowledge that there is someone who would be willing to discuss such issues. Individual or group counseling for some fraternity men may facilitate such changing awareness.

In addition, there is the concern of sexual orientation on the part of fraternity men. Those members of fraternities who are gay or bisexual also struggle in an environment that is not only traditionally male but homophobic as well. The denial of the existence of gay men in fraternities adds further strain to the gay or bisexual men already struggling with the previously mentioned issues while trying to live in a primarily male environment. Student services professionals working with such men in Greek organizations must then be aware of the needs of these students and how they might work to educate this possibly resistant subpopulation of changing men.

Male Paraprofessionals

Men who serve the campus as paraprofessionals—for example, resident advisers (RAs), peer counselors, learning/study skills workers, career development assistants—are potential role models for other students. The potential exists to affect many male students by working with campus paraprofessionals to assist them in becoming more aware of the issues involved in gender role strain and conflict and then having them share their knowledge and awareness with others. Most paraprofessionals are usually quite visible on campus, often show their dedication through long hours of service, and are frequently willing to work with other groups on campus in addition to their designated roles.

Male paraprofessionals are very busy, as their jobs on campus may be only a part of their daily routine. They are also students, may hold down another job, and will need to find time to study and play. Men who are RAs are painfully aware of living in a "fishbowl" environment, being available twenty-four hours a day and having little privacy. Male RAs are not only role models in general to students living in on-campus residences but also to those students who share living space with the RA and are viewed as his "charges." While RA training usually addresses the issue of the student being a role model, it is most often in the context of alcohol use, visitation by females, and upholding university policies and regulations. Rarely does this training include discussion of gender role strain, sex role stereotyping, and sexism. And yet the RA may have the opportunity to have more impact on new students than any other particular individual on campus, especially during a new student's first year (Blimling and Miltenberger, 1984).

Interventions for paraprofessionals include, for example, training RAs specifically about sexism and the issues of gender role strain. Other paraprofessionals may benefit from similar training, and a number of campuses across the country have developed paraprofessional training programs for students to become group and discussion leaders on such topics as human sexuality, career development, and responsible sexuality. The material presented for training students could easily be adapted to include gender role issues (not only for the men, but for the women paraprofessionals as well).

Male Student Leaders

It is important to review some of the information and discuss another group of men who are potential role models for a campus environment—male student leaders (that is, student government leaders, student liaisons to faculty committees, and so on). Like paraprofessionals, they are extremely busy and committed to the work that they do. They tend to be more traditional when compared to their more androgynous RA counterparts, and they have probably received less training than RAs. But it is their being visible on campus and their potential for being role models of changing men in higher education that warrants their inclusion in this chapter.

Male student leaders have been found to see themselves as more successful than other students (Schuh and Laverty, 1983). They appear to both remember these experiences positively and to view their student leadership role as having a permanent effect on their lives (Downey, Bosco, and Silver, 1984). And yet many male leaders are perceived by their fellow students as being interested only in the power that comes with the office, in getting another line on their résumé to impress employment recruiters, or in impressing women. Additionally, some (if not many) male student leaders are also members of fraternities and share the concerns described above. Since many student leaders are often overcommitted and overextended in their daily lives, perhaps intervention could center on the issues of men's health concerns, stress and time management, and how the competitive spirit may take over their lives without warning and awareness.

As mentioned previously, issues of gender role strain and conflict can be discussed with student leaders either directly—as a topic presented to student leaders in their leadership training seminars—or indirectly in the context of seminars for leaders that also look at time and stress management while discussing other concerns that would affect their performance as leaders and students. The reader should keep in mind, again, that many (though clearly not all) male student leaders are quite traditional, especially in their views of the role of men and women, and may in fact be quite resistant to hearing how their roles need to change (Dickerson and Hester, 1982).

Adult Male Students

This final subpopulation includes men who have already begun to challenge the stereotypes of men in American society as they choose to return to school (or perhaps to begin higher education) after a number of years in the workforce or military, or men who choose to receive a college education or advanced degree and have a spouse who is also committed to a career. While there are differences between these two groups of men, there also exists a great deal of similarity. The men are often older than the traditional eighteen- to twenty-two-year-old college male, they generally share a greater number of years of life and work experience, and they may both be viewed as "odd" by traditional students (Dickerson and Hester, 1982). They have often experienced life as traditional men, with traditional roles and expectations (Cherpas, 1985). Retired military men who now are entering or returning to college have experienced gender role strain and conflict in their lives as military personnel. Some adult male students want an education to provide them with another set of skills, while others want a new way of looking at life.

Often with children, frequently divorced, and dissatisfied with their career experiences, adult male students often seek the advice and encouragement of other men to follow through on their desire to change. Many campuses across the country have developed programs for women returning to school (for example, the displaced homemaker programs found in many community colleges and vocational and technical schools, as well as programs at colleges and universities that attempt to help the returning student adjust to a new way of life). Some institutions have expanded these services for men as well; they find that men and women can share their concerns of fear, academic performance expectations, and how to deal with their spouses and/or children as they change the course of their lives. Support groups for these men (sometimes called men in transition) provide a supportive environment that allows men to share their fears, seek and provide support for other men experiencing similar struggles, and perhaps build a new set of friends who understand the dilemmas of the traditional man (Washington, 1982).

Men in dual-career relationships find themselves in a situation that challenges them to make decisions jointly with their partner instead of, as traditional males, deciding on their own and telling their partner what they have decided. Such men very quickly experience gender role strain and conflict as they work to make the decision to leave a career or job and pursue an education. Often the loss of income creates a crisis for the couple or family that can be anticipated, but the feelings cannot be predicted. Many men in dual-career relationships see pursuing an education as the struggle, and when they finish school life will be much better. But the completion of an education sometimes only leads to the next, perhaps even more difficult, decision—a possible geographic move as the result of one or both partners advancing, changing careers or employers. Traditional relationships where the wife or partner either doesn't work or has a job (as opposed to the commitment of a career) allow the man to make the decision about where he and his partner will go. In dual-career relationships, it is a joint decision weighing the benefits and costs to both careers, thus making the decision that much more difficult (Parker, Peltier, and Wolleat, 1981; Amatea and Cross, 1983; Cherpas, 1985).

Interventions with men in dual-career relationships can also begin with support—in the form of organized groups, informal discussions, and so on. Adult male students should be encouraged to get involved with those groups designed to assist them. If such groups do not exist, they should be started by student services professionals. Another positive way to impact adult male students is to assist them in finding male role models on campus—finding a mentor may be the most powerful intervention possible. On most campuses there exist male faculty and staff who have been adult learners themselves, or there are men who have been "in transition." When solicited, these men are often willing to lend support on an informal basis. One such program on a campus is a weekly support group that includes faculty, staff, and adult male students that meets to discuss issues that occur, to assist in problem solving, and to provide support.

For men in dual-career relationships, it is important to offer the provision of services to the spouse as well (Amatea and Cross, 1983; Amatea and Clark, 1984). A number of dual-career assistance programs are being offered through the offices of career planning and placement services, in addition to short-term counseling services. Men in dual-career relationships often need and desire encouragement to break with traditional expectations and to be able to respond appropriately to possible attacks from other men about their masculinity as a result of jointly making decisions with their partner. Men may be ridiculed because their wives may be supporting the family while they are in school or because a career change might result in their partners earning more money than they do. Men in dual-career relationships, who may be the role model for this and the next generation of college students (Gilbert, 1987), need the encouragement of student services professionals who support the changing roles of men and women in society.

Comments on Intervention

The reader should be aware of the importance of choosing not only the most appropriate intervention for a particular subpopulation but also the level of that intervention, the method of delivery, and the evaluation of these efforts. In a classic article, Morrill, Oetting, and Hurst (1974) describe three dimensions (the "Cube" model) that can be used to determine the most effective purpose, method, and target of an intervention. In this chapter, the following interventions have been encouraged, and they provide samples of those types of interventions described in the Morrill, Oetting, and Hurst article.

• Individual counseling (voluntary/disciplinary): used for the resolution of personal problems with an emphasis on how the male student is affected by the issues of gender role strain and conflict (for example, gay and bisexual men, adult male students) (Good and May, 1987)

• Men's support and consciousness-raising groups: used to assist specific groups of men with common concerns to build a support network (for example, international males, adult male students, gay and bisexual males), or to bring diverse groups of men together to share concerns about how the traditional male role is negatively affecting their lives (Washington, 1982; Rabinowitz and Cochran, 1987)

• Teaching and training: developing programs that seek to expand knowledge and awareness of men's issues on campus but may also share other focuses (for example, responsible sexuality workshops for residence halls students, guest lectures in classes, leadership development workshops for student leaders)

• Campus-wide educational programming: creating opportunities on campus to develop visible public arenas to educate students about men's issues through invited lectures, debates, or a series of programs to describe the effects of traditional male roles on both men and women (for example, men's awareness day, gender roles awareness programs, men's awareness week).

Training of Student Services Professionals and Staffs

Indirect, but significant, programming on campus that occurs through the training of staff in student services about men's issues will increase awareness of gender role issues, and through these programs will influence the climate of the campus. In addition, student services professionals who are more aware of these concerns could be more sensitive to the needs of male students and ultimately provide better services to both male and female students on campus.

The progression of involvement on a campus in programming for men's issues might develop this way: lectures about men's concerns, men's awareness week on campus, regular programming about men's issues and concerns, the development of a men's center on campus, men's studies academic programs (for example, the University of Southern California's program on the Study of Women and Men in Society). Student services professionals who decide to conduct men's programming on campus should be aware of the needs of various student subpopulations and the method of delivering programs that provide the greatest effectiveness.

Summary

This chapter has described seven groups of men considered special populations on college and university campuses. The specific issues and needs of each group of men were discussed as well as possible interventions. The role of student services in assisting these changing men on our campuses will be a significant component to success.

References

Amatea, E., and Clark, J. "A Dual Career Workshop for College Couples: Effects of an Intervention Program." *Journal of College Student Personnel*, 1984, *25*, 271-272.

Amatea, E., and Cross, E. G. "Coupling and Careers: A Workshop for Dual Career Couples at the Launching Stage." *Personnel and Guidance Journal*, 1983, *62*, 48-52.

Anderson, T. R., and Myer, T. E. "Presenting Problems, Counselor Contacts, and 'no shows': International and American College Students." *Journal of College Student Personnel*, 1985, *26*, 500-503.

Bausch-Altman, E., and Whitner, P. "Study Skills for Student Athletes." *Journal of College Student Personnel*, 1986, *27*, 369-370.

Blann, F. W. "Intercollegiate Athletic Competition and Students' Educational and Career Plans." *Journal of College Student Personnel*, 1985, *25*, 115-118.

Blimling, G. S., and Miltenberger, L. J. *The Resident Assistant: Working with College Students in Residence Halls*. Dubuque, Iowa: Kendall/Hunt, 1984.

Cherpas, C. C. "Dual-Career Families: Terminology, Typologies, and Work and Family Issues." *Journal of Counseling and Development*, 1985, *63*, 616-619.

Coleman, E. "Developmental Stages of the Coming Out Process." In J. C. Gonsiorek (ed.), *Homosexuality and Psychotherapy: A Practitioner's Handbook of Affirmative Models*. New York: Haworth Press, 1981.

Dadfar, S., and Friedlander, M. L. "Differential Attitudes of International Students Toward Seeking Professional Psychological Help." *Journal of Counseling Psychology*, 1982, *29* (3), 335-338.

Davis, L. "Racial Issues in the Training of Group Workers." *Journal for Specialists in Group Work*, 1981, *6*, 155-170.

Dickerson, K., and Hester, S. "The Emerging Dual-Career Life-Style: Are Your Students Prepared for It?" *Journal of College Student Personnel*, 1982, *23*, 514-519.

Downey, R. G., Bosco, P. J., and Silver, E. M. "Long-Term Outcomes of Participation in Student Government." *Journal of College Student Personnel*, 1984, *25*, 245-250.

Fradkin, H. "Counseling Men in the AIDS Crisis." In M. Scher, M. Stevens, G. Good, and G. Eichenfield (eds.), *Handbook of Counseling and Psychotherapy with Men.* Newbury Park, Calif.: Sage, 1987.

Gilbert, L. A. "Women and Men Together but Equal: Issues for Men in Dual Career Marriages." In M. Scher, M. Stevens, G. Good, and G. Eichenfield (eds.), *Handbook of Counseling and Psychotherapy of Men.* Newbury Park, Calif.: Sage, 1987.

Good, G., and May, R. "Developmental Issues, Environmental Influences, and the Nature of Therapy with College Men." In M. Scher, M. Stevens, G. Good, and G. Eichenfield (eds.), *Handbook of Counseling and Psychotherapy with Men.* Newbury Park, Calif.: Sage, 1987.

Greer, R. M., and Moore, T. "Athletics and Academics: One Student Affairs Effort." *Journal of College Student Personnel,* 1986, *27,* 572.

Gressard, C. F., and Sowa, C. "Athletic Participation: Its Relationship to Student Development." *Journal of College Student Personnel,* 1983, *24,* 236-239.

Gunnison, H. "Group Work with Athletes." *Journal for Specialists in Group Work,* 1985, *10* (4), 211-216.

Harrison, J. "Counseling Gay Men." In M. Scher, M. Stevens, G. Good, and G. Eichenfield (eds.), *Handbook of Counseling and Psychotherapy with Men.* Newbury Park, Calif.: Sage, 1987.

Harrison, R. E. "Psychosocial Dimensions of Student Athletes: Implications for Developmental Studies." *Personnel and Guidance Journal,* 1981, *60,* 113-115.

Henderson, G., and Weber, J. C. *College Survival Skills for Student-Athletes.* Springfield, Ill.: Thomas, 1985.

Hirt, J., Hoffman, M., and Sedlacek, W. "Attitudes Toward Changing Sex-Roles of Male Varsity Athletes Versus Nonathletes: Developmental Perspectives." *Journal of College Student Personnel,* 1983, *24,* 33-38.

"Is the Dream Over?" *Newsweek on Campus,* February 1987, pp. 10-22.

Lara-Cantu, M. A., and Navarro-Arias, R. "Positive and Negative Factors in the Measurement of Sex Roles: Findings from a Mexican Sample." *Hispanic Journal of Behavioral Sciences,* 1986, *8* (2), 143-155.

Lee, C. C. "An Investigation of the Athletic Career Expectations of High School Student Athletes." *Personnel and Guidance Journal,* 1983, *61,* 544-547.

Lee, C. C. "Black Manhood Training: Group Counseling for Male Blacks in Grades 7-12." *Journal for Specialists in Group Work,* 1987, *12* (1), 18-25.

Lee, D. B., and Saul, T. T. "Counseling Asian Men." In M. Scher, M. Stevens, G. Good, and G. Eichenfield (eds.), *Handbook of Counseling and Psychotherapy with Men.* Newbury Park, Calif.: Sage, 1987.

Leong, F., and Sedlacek, W. E. *Comparison of International and U.S. Students' Preference for Helping Sources.* Research Report No. 1-85. College Park: Counseling Center, University of Maryland, 1985.

Malyon, A. K. "Psychotherapeutic Implications of Internalized Homophobia in Gay Men." In J. C. Gonsiorek (ed.), *Homosexuality and Psychotherapy: A Practitioner's Handbook of Affirmative Models.* New York: Haworth Press, 1981.

Manese, J. E., Sedlacek, W. E., and Leong, F. "Needs and Perceptions of Female and Male Undergraduate Students." *College Student Affairs Journal,* 1985, *6,* 19-28.

Morrill, W. H., Oetting, E. R., and Hurst, J. C. "Dimensions of Counselor Functioning." *Personnel and Guidance Journal,* 1974, *52,* 354-360.

NCAA *1987-88 Manual of the National Collegiate Athletic Association.* Mission, Kans.: NCAA, 1987.

Orlofsky, J. L. "Identity Formation, Achievement, and Fear of Success in College Men and Women." *Journal of Youth and Adolescence,* 1978, 7 (1), 49-62.

Parker, M., Peltier, S., and Wolleat, P. "Understanding Dual Career Couples." *Personnel and Guidance Journal,* 1981, *60,* 14–18.

Perkins, C. S., Perkins, M. L., Guglielmino, L. M., and Reiff, R. F. "A Comparison of the Adjustment Problems of Three International Student Groups." *Journal of College Student Personnel,* 1977, *18* (5), 382–388.

Rabinowitz, F., and Cochran, S. "Counseling Men in Groups." In M. Scher, M. Stevens, G. Good, and G. Eichenfield (eds.), *Handbook of Counseling and Psychotherapy with Men.* Newbury Park, Calif.: Sage, 1987.

Schuh, J. H., and Laverty, M. "The Perceived Long-Term Influence of Holding a Significant Student Leadership Position." *Journal of College Student Personnel,* 1983, *24,* 28–32.

Valdez, L., Baron, A., and Ponce, F. "Counseling Hispanic Men." In M. Scher, M. Stevens, G. Good, and G. Eichenfield (eds.), *Handbook of Counseling and Psychotherapy with Men.* Newbury Park, Calif.: Sage, 1987.

Washington, C. S. "Challenging Men in Groups." *Journal for Specialists in Group Work,* 1982, 7, 132–136.

Wittmer, J., Bostic, D., Phillips, T. D., and Waters, W. "The Personal, Academic, and Career Problems of College Student Athletes: Some Possible Answers." *Personnel and Guidance Journal,* 1981, *60,* 52–59.

Gregg A. Eichenfield is associate director of the University of Oklahoma Counseling Center. Aside from gender role issues, his interests include paraprofessional training, suicide issues, and counseling gay and lesbian clients.

Colleges and universities can implement programs that
effectively promote awareness and growth in the lives of
male students.

Developmental Programs

Fred Leafgren

This chapter addresses the importance and value of developmental programs for male students enrolled in institutions of higher education. Information, strategies, and resources for men's awareness programming are provided, the use and value of assessments are discussed, topics and programs on men's issues are identified, and strategies for communicating men's issues are suggested.

Because gender roles have been changing for several years, programs specifically oriented to men are long overdue on college and university campuses. Most college students today anticipate and look forward to opportunities for growth and change during their college years, even though they may not clearly perceive those opportunities. Men, in particular, need to participate in programs that can provide assistance in their development.

Problems with Programming on Male Issues

The importance of developing programs on men's issues should not be minimized simply because initial student response and participation levels may be low. Various reasons can account for a slow start.

Levels of Awareness. Students come to college and universities in different shapes and sizes, in different phases of development. For example, male students working hard to establish a male identity may have

R. J. May and M. Scher (eds.). *Changing Roles for Men on Campus.*
New Directions for Student Services, no. 42. San Francisco: Jossey-Bass, Summer 1988.

little inclination to confront issues of masculinity. Their big concern at this stage is to be recognized as male, both by females and other males. Other male students are eager to confront issues related to their total development, and still others passed the masculine identity issue long ago and are now working on issues of marriage, parenting, and single parenthood. Programs can be planned for a variety of audiences.

Levels of Acceptance. While society is changing rapidly, some individuals are slow to accept change—especially where personal beliefs and values are concerned.

Today, men's and women's roles are significantly different from those of their ancestors. For this reason, it is important to provide individuals with the knowledge and skills they need to function at an optimal level in their changing environment. Exploring our past can help us understand the present. Such exploration involves recognizing and understanding the family system and role expectations that we grew up with, and then understanding how that system and those expectations affect our attitudes. It also involves becoming aware of the changing roles and expectations for men and women.

Changing Roles. Historically, men have been rewarded for being self-sufficient and competitive, while women have been praised for being caring and expressive. Today, such traditional roles have become less clearly defined. Women are moving from the more nurturing, caring roles to the more independent, competitive roles. They are taking charge. This change often leaves men confused about their own roles and the relationship of their roles to women's roles.

Men need to explore their self-images. They need to understand how self-images affect relationships with others and how changing the self-image can change a relationship. However, men attempting to change the stereotypical male role must recognize that not all men and women are choosing to leave the traditional roles behind. Some are resistant to all change, while others accept various levels of change. The resulting spectrum of changing roles adds to an already confusing situation. Men are put in the position of having to cope with widely different role-related behavior (not only between the sexes, but also among the sexes) and the conflicts associated with these divergent life-styles.

Programming for Diverse Needs

People involved with developing any new program on a college campus need to recognize the diversity of the audience and the variety of responses that may be encountered. Eventually, many students will become involved in such programs if they are provided with the opportunity to do so in a safe, comfortable environment.

Kelly (1976) identified three distinct types of men who are emerging:

1. The *new masculinist,* who enjoys sharing in the atmosphere of equality, finding it liberating, refreshing, and manageable. He sees women as sexual equals and is free to share his spectrum of emotions with others.
2. The *male traditionalist,* who feels more comfortable in the dominant role of guide, protector, and provider for women. He tends to believe that men should be the sexual aggressors, that they should appear strong and controlled as well as controlling, and that double standardism is legitimate.
3. The *mediator male,* who attempts to straddle both worlds. His attitudes toward sexuality tend to follow a somewhat opportunistic path of convenience and manageability.

The new masculinist male and the mediator male may be more responsive to programs on male issues than the male traditionalist, who has broad-based societal support and may be less inclined than the others to become introspective about the male role and its impact on total emotional and physical well-being. However, the male traditionalist can benefit from programs on male issues and should be included in the target audience when such programs are being developed.

Significant priorities and issues for various types of men should be identified and programs should be designed to address them. For instance, the new masculinist male will likely be responsive to programs on the changing role of males and the emerging issues that accompany new male roles. The emotional, social, physical, spiritual, and occupational implications of such change can serve as program thrusts. The male traditionalist is more likely to respond to programs that identify the differences in male and female roles. His willingness to discuss and explore these differences may open up opportunities to begin to introduce changes occurring in traditional female roles and the implications these will have for the traditional male. The mediator male is likely to be willing to explore the changing roles of men and women, and the anticipated behavior and life-style changes required.

Kelly confirms my view that regardless of their place in the male scheme of things, men will experience turmoil and problems during this important period of change and growth in contemporary sexual values and roles. Colleges and universities can assist men in anticipating potential problems as well as in identifying possible solutions.

Assessing Needs of Male Students

Assessment can provide opportunities to gather data, establish group norms, and obtain information about needs with regard to present life-styles, concerns, interests, attitudes, and beliefs. This information is essential to a solidly based program and can be very helpful in planning individual programs to meet needs and clarify existing beliefs, attitudes, and opinions. Institutions of higher education are familiar and comfortable with this approach for many institutional activities and programs.

Value of Assessment to Individual. In the case of men's issues, the value of assessment is much greater than that of merely assessing and obtaining group data. I have identified four major values of the assessment process for the individual, as follows:

1. A consciousness-raising experience for men about men's issues. It raises questions and concerns in the individual's mind that previously might not have been evident.
2. Increased clarification about the individual's present life-style, attitudes, opinions, beliefs, and behaviors. This information helps individuals respond to the choices available as they make decisions about changes in their life-styles.
3. Expanded knowledge of life-style choices. For each of us, knowledge of the world around us has been limited by our family, community, religious, and cultural orientation. We frequently deny ourselves excellent opportunities for growth simply because we are not aware of the options. The assessment process often provides information about choices we were unaware of.
4. Stimulation for participation in men's programs. The process of completing assessment instruments frequently stimulates an individual's desire or need to receive information and feedback about his or her responses, how those responses compare to the responses of others, and how her or his life-style compares to norm or peer groups. This stimulation frequently leads an individual to further explore and inquire about issues of interest. When that happens, the demand for programs related to those issues increases.

Assessment Instruments. The early measures of gender identity lack utility because they are based upon a bipolar view of gender identity. Today's concept of androgyny assumes an individual can possess both masculine and feminine attributes, in contrast to masculinity and femininity being viewed as opposite ends of a continuum. At least three instruments are available with scales for masculinity, femininity, and androgyny. All three instruments have been found to have construct validity and test/retest reliabilities of at least 0.81 (Boles and Tatro, 1982).

The Bem Sex Role Inventory (Bem, 1974) was the initial measure of androgyny. The sixty items equally represent traits rated as desirable for a man, woman, or neutral. Although androgyny was originally defined as the difference between masculine and feminine scores, Bem now favors scoring using a median split method derived by Spence, Helmreich, and Stapp (1975). Those scoring above the masculine and feminine means are identified as androgynous, while those below both means are considered undifferentiated.

The same scoring scheme is used with the fifty-five-item Personal Attributes Questionnaire (Spence and Helmreich, 1978). Individuals rate themselves on items chosen for their social desirability and prevalence in either gender. A short form of twenty-four items is also available with a 0.90 correlation between forms.

The PRF ANDRO (Berzins, Welling, and Wetter, 1978) is a fifty-six-item true-false instrument derived from Murray's need theory. Masculine items reflect ascendancy, autonomy, and risk taking. Feminine items reflect nurturance, affiliation, expression, and self-subordination.

Another instrument that may prove useful for men's programming is the Attitudes Toward Women Scale (Spence and Helmreich, 1972). This fifteen-item rating scale measures attitudes toward the rights and roles of women in society.

Men's Issues for Developmental Programs

Because programming in the area of men's issues is relatively new, it might seem to some that there are not a great many topics to discuss. On the contrary; there are numerous and varied issues to address, such as:

- Male relationships: can include communication of feelings, power and control, men and friendship, intimacy, homophobia, father-son relationships, and relationships with the opposite sex
- Emotional development: can include anger, awareness of feelings, love, vulnerability, aloneness, loneliness, self-esteem, guilt, emotional support, and mental health
- Sexual activity: can include attitudes about sexuality, sexually transmitted diseases, contraception, and date rape
- Male role within our culture: can include the effect of the college experience on being male, being hypermasculine, cooperation and independence, experiences of growing up male, men's gender roles, being feminine, success and achievement, men's culture, and what is normal
- Male-female relationships: can include communication of feelings, power and control, mother-son relationships, friendships, intimacy, perceptions of women, men competing with women, and friendship relationships
- Social relationships: can include pornography, crime, date rape, violence, gay rights, and sexist language and its impact on how people think
- Marriage and family: can include men and children; alternatives to traditional marriage; marriage, divorce, and child custody; and love
- Health: can include physical health, physical activity, nutrition, drugs, sexually transmitted diseases, and death and dying
- Spiritual values: can include the entire valuing concept.

All of these topics relate to significant developmental issues that can be of interest and concern to men and can lead to significant personal growth.

A comprehensive review of the literature on men's issues was prepared in 1986 by the Committee on Men of the American Association for Counseling and Development. (The bibliography, updated annually, can be obtained from the AACD Headquarters, 5999 Stevenson Avenue, Alexandria, Virginia, 22304.)

Strategies for Enhancing Men's Awareness of Issues on Male Development

Strategies for enhancing men's awareness and facilitating men's development include small-group participation, workshops, support groups, offices of men's services, academic services, and media. In the following paragraphs, each of these will be discussed and appropriate programs will be suggested for each type of intervention.

Small Group Participation. Programs should be designed for small-groups, ideally composed of no more than eight to ten individuals. This does not deny the importance of presenting programs on men's issues to large audiences. However, small groups maximize the opportunity for exploration, sharing, and intervention and, therefore, are better suited to this type of program. In addition, small groups allow for flexibility in choice of topic and type of presentation. Such programs might include:

• "What Does It Mean to Be a Man?" which asks participants to share with the group those characteristics they feel are important attributes of the male role. They are encouraged to try to identify the sources from which their attitudes and beliefs come, to challenge one another when there are differences of opinion, and to evaluate the assets and liabilities of each characteristic in terms of the impact on their own growth, development, and capacity to relate to members of both the opposite sex and the same sex.

• "Lies I Use to Prove My Masculinity," which encourages participants to identify lies they use in attempting to prove their masculinity to females and other males. They are encouraged to reflect on the impact these lies have on their own development in relationship building and to think about how they use lies to communicate personal characteristics not truly representative of their personalities. Often these lies are used to conceal perceived weaknesses and are barriers to relationship building.

• The use of songs that talk about growing up male, which can stimulate thinking and discussion. These might include "Cats in the Cradle" by Harry Chapin, "William Wants a Doll" by Marlo Thomas and Alan Alda, "Macho Man" by the Village People, "Born Free" by

John Barry, and "Kodachrome," "I Am a Rock," and "Bookends" by Simon and Garfunkel. Such songs raise issues regarding sex roles and masculinity and can be used very effectively in small-group consciousness-raising and discussion.

• Films and videos such as *An Acquired Taste* (Arlyck, 1982), a twenty-six-minute film that looks at school, work, and media influences that shaped Arlyck's life and, he believes, the lives of all men. The film poses critical questions about forces that fuel the pursuit of success and deals with such topics as American values of male roles, growing up, career success, and life-styles. Another good choice is *Welcome Home, Bobby*, a CBS presentation about a teenager trying to come to terms with his sexual identity. Both films lend themselves to discussion following presentation. Other visual media sources are included in the references at the end of this sourcebook. These always provide stimulation for consciousness-raising and discussion, and serve as strong catalysts for programs.

There are many potential topics suitable for small-group participation and discussion (a number of these are listed in the next section of this chapter). However, I want to reiterate that the small-group approach has many advantages, with one of the strongest being the opportunity to build trust among group participants to maximize sharing, mutual disclosure, and personal growth. The importance of building trust cannot be overemphasized.

Workshops. The big advantage of workshops designed for programs on men's issues and men's development is the time they allow for exploring topics in greater depth. Workshops conducted at retreat facilities, away from the participants' regular environments, usually work best. This setting frees participants from daily routines and pressures and encourages greater introspection and sharing. It is important to select a focus, set program plans and goals, and communicate all this information to prospective participants before they commit to the workshop. Failure to do this may result in expectations not being met and disruption of the workshop by participants who expected something different.

Allow adequate time for planning the workshop so that it is organized and structured to provide an optimal experience for participants. Whether the workshop is planned and presented by professionals or by the participants themselves, it still requires careful planning. Specific goals and accomplishments will not be met by simply having a group of individuals get together without any structure or plan to follow.

The following suggestions for workshops illustrate the possibilities for programs. There are many others.

Human Sexuality. Workshops on human sexuality are typically popular among college-age students. They provide a forum for inquiry and promote further personal identification and understanding of sexuality. While such workshops may take a variety of formats, one approach is to introduce students to variations of human sexuality through the use of media sources and then to help them clarify their own sexual roles and behaviors while understanding and becoming more tolerant of behaviors that differ from theirs. A weekend should provide ample time for discussion, mutual sharing, support, and reflection on the issues.

Loneliness. The topic of loneliness has relevance for all students, but men may need to take a harder look at how they cope with loneliness in contrast to how women cope. In addition to identifying how they experience and cope with loneliness, men can benefit from learning ways of coping that are more emotionally healthy.

Sexually Transmitted Diseases. With the current epidemic of AIDS threatening virtually everyone today, workshops on sexually transmitted diseases are very important. Students must learn how to protect themselves from becoming infected, and they must understand the impact such diseases can have on their lives. At the present time, our only defense against AIDS is education.

Love and Marriage. Workshops focused on love and marriage are well attended. Young people of college age are concerned with issues about love and marriage, so this is certainly a topic for both males and females. However, a workshop allowing men to explore their particular concerns can be very helpful to them. I believe that having a greater self-awareness of what he or she wants in a relationship and expects in a marriage (as it relates to intimacy, passion, and commitment) will make it easier for an individual to choose a partner and may lead to a more stable marital relationship.

Opposite Sex. Workshops in which men and women jointly explore issues and concerns they share about members of the opposite sex are usually popular and often result in significant growth for both sexes. They begin to understand better the expectations, interests, and needs of members of the opposite sex; communication is usually enhanced; and discussion of previously unshared topics is stimulated.

Friendships. Workshops focusing on friends, friendship relationships, and the dimensions of friendship relationships can facilitate growth for men in an area that is often very difficult for them. Men's relationships are frequently based on action-oriented involvement in projects, sports, and activities. There is little sharing of feelings and attitudes, and little open discussion about trust, love, and mutual support. Usually these feelings exist but are not verbalized. Friendship workshops can facilitate the communication of such significant issues and enhance friendship relationships between members of the opposite sex, too. Workshops that deal with competition between men and women are timely because of the increasing number of women assuming roles in the workplace and in athletics that, historically, have been male dominated.

Exploring ways for men to appreciate and become more sensitive to women in these arenas can provide a real workshop challenge.

Spirituality and Sexuality. Workshops on spirituality and sexuality provide opportunities for men to explore their spiritual and sexual roles, and to understand how these interrelate. Moral issues and relationships can also be discussed. James Nelson (1985), in his article "Male Sexuality and Masculine Spirituality," explores this topic in some depth.

Father-Son Relationships. A good way to set the stage for a workshop on father-son relationships is to use an article that appeared in the September/October 1986 issue of the *New Age Journal.* Entitled "Father Hunger: The Secret Wound of American Men" (Merton, 1986), it explores how father-son relationships affect men. Discussion may awaken old, unresolved issues that need attention so that individuals can move forward into healthy relationships with their own children. The potential for gaining significant insight and understanding is great.

Stress. Learning ways of coping with stress provides a popular and therapeutic topic for a workshop. Specific activities can be included to teach individuals how to deal with daily stress.

Men's Heroes, Role Models, and Mentors. The ways in which male identity has been shaped are explored in workshops on heroes, role models, and mentors. Participants can reassess their own identities and real capabilities versus those they may have adopted from their heroes, role models, and mentors.

Any of these topics can serve as a basis for workshops, small-group programs, or large-group presentations. An assessment of the needs and interests of a specific college population can give direction to those programs and workshops most likely to be of interest and in which participation is most likely to occur.

Ongoing Support Groups. Fraternities, athletic teams, residence halls, other living groups, social clubs, and other social activities have provided support systems in the past. Ongoing support groups are more likely to provide in-depth experiences when small groups of individuals commit to work with one another on shared concerns over a period of time sufficient to allow trust, intimacy, and close relationships to develop.

Such groups not only provide immediate support within the group but also can enhance present and future relationships with both sexes outside the group. Groups may select trained leaders, and they may choose to have shared leadership. Whatever the group decides, its expectations and goals should be clearly identified and agreed upon by all participants.

Ongoing support groups may be outgrowths of programs, workshops, or other existing groups in which there is already an established relationship, even though it is not as focused and intensive as is possible in an ongoing support group. It takes time to build trust, in-depth sharing, intimacy, and friendship. The process cannot be rushed, but it can be facilitated by trained leaders and participants who have common goals and expectations, and who have comparable levels of experience and maturity.

The outcomes for such groups suggest that the experience can be extremely rewarding and can produce much growth. Individuals who have participated in support groups report that they have experienced enhanced communication with individuals of both sexes, greater personal self-fulfillment, increased self-awareness, and greater satisfaction in their daily lives. Stein (1982) and Rabinowitz and Cochran (1987) provide two excellent sources of information about men's support groups.

Office of Men's Services. Women's resource centers, offices for women's studies, and other offices focusing on programs designed especially for women can be found on many campuses across this country. They have become an expected and rather typical part of college life. But what about offices for men's resources, men's studies, men's support? Well, the fact is, they are not so typical. However, a few do exist. For example, at the University of Massachusetts, the Men's Center (Hamlin Dorm, University of Massachusetts–Amherst, Amherst, Mass. 01003) provides resources and materials, and promotes programs for men. At the University of Southern California (Paper Hall-331M, USC, Los Angeles, Calif. 90089-4352), "The Study of Women and Men in Society" is an ongoing program dealing with a variety of issues.

Such offices could be very helpful in (1) forming groups for men against sexual assault, men against violence, and men interested in supporting long-range educational and community projects or projects directed toward men; (2) extending their services outside the university setting and helping others to make contributions that would have a significant impact on existing community cultures; and (3) providing media and library resources, program ideas, workshops, programs that bring individuals with common interests together, and services specifically oriented toward men and men's issues.

Academic Courses. Some colleges and universities are now offering courses in men's issues. The examples offered here might be used as models for developing such courses.

- The University of Wisconsin–Milwaukee offers "Male Identity: Education and Development."
- The YMCA at the University of Illinois offers a credit course through the university called "Men's Support and Awareness Group." Men gather weekly to "talk things out." It is reported that the most commonly discussed topics include intimate relationship problems, troubles in job situations, and problems with children and parents.
- The University of Illinois offers "Human Sexuality 206."

Reported to be one of the most popular courses offered, it gives
students an objective view of sex from which they can form
values, even though the course is not specifically designed to
change student attitudes.

Courses such as these should be encouraged and promoted on college
and university campuses. The need is there, the issues are real, and the
impact on the individual can be very powerful.

Media. There are many excellent media sources on men's issues.
(See Chapter Seven, "Resources for Promoting Change in Men's Lives,"
for a partial listing of such sources.) Establishing a library of such materials in a men's center or at various other locations on campus where
they will be easily accessible is important in the effort to raise awareness
levels. A university bookstore or any bookstore that serves the student
population should be contacted about and encouraged to stock significant books and newly released books on men's issues.

Marketing Strategies for Men's Issues Programming

Although it is often overlooked, the marketing aspect of developing any program is vital to the program's success. No matter how good a
program is, it can't be successful if no one shows up, and people can't
show up if they don't know about it. Campus newspapers, radio stations,
television productions, and bulletin boards are all important avenues for
the dissemination and promotion of information. Every avenue of promotion should be used.

Often, those people most interested in developing the programs
are not interested in marketing them, so it is important to identify individuals early in the program development process who have skills and an
interest in marketing. Overlooking this important aspect of programming
can lead to poor attendance at and participation in programs, and that
can lead to discouragement for those who spent time planning the program (and may even have an effect on the continued promotion of the
issue involved).

While I do not propose to focus on the steps involved in marketing, it is important to emphasize the need for marketing skills in the
promotion of programs dealing with men's issues and men's development. Often, when questions are raised about what gets men to attend
programs, the response is: "Anything about sex or birth control, and
anything that is funny." But, programs dealing with issues about which
men feel inadequate and programs offering help in areas where men feel
a need will also get a good response if promoted well. An excellent video-
tape on campus publicity entitled *Against All Odds* (Harris, 1987) has
recently been made available.

64

Conclusion

People are constantly evolving and changing throughout their lives. They build, rearrange the pieces, and incorporate material. Often, they do this without understanding the "building material" choices and alternatives available. What they choose to incorporate into their physical, emotional, and psychological makeup determines the way in which they respond to their world and themselves.

Men need to know the alternatives available to them. They need to learn to give up control, to communicate in the language of feeling, to discover their own feelings, and to express intimacy in nonsexual terms. They also need to learn how to develop friendships with other males and how to deal more effectively with power issues.

Traditional American male role expectations deny choices and opportunities for self-discovery and interpersonal fulfillment to many, if not most, college-age male students. Gender role exploration is a critical issue. Failure to recognize the issues related to being male in our society and making personal decisions for oneself interferes with emotional, social, and career development. Anxiety and frustration about male identity and related issues can also have an impact upon one's intellectual and spiritual well-being.

Administrators, counselors, and educators have a responsibility to provide and support programs that encourage and facilitate healthy male development. When men's issues are overlooked, both men and women are the losers.

References

Arlyck, R. *An Acquired Taste.* Wayne, N.J.: New Day Films, 1982. Film.

Bem, S. L. "Measurement of Psychology Androgyny." *Journal of Consulting and Clinical Psychology,* 1974, *42,* 55–162.

Berzins, J., Welling, M., and Wetter, R. "A New Measure of Psychological Androgyny Based on the Personal Research Form." *Journal of Consulting and Clinical Psychology,* 1978, *46,* 126–128.

Boles, J., and Tatro, C. "Androgyny." In K. Solomon and N. B. Levy (eds.), *Men in Transition: Theory and Therapy.* New York: Plenum Press, 1982.

Farrell, W. *Why Men Are the Way They Are.* New York: McGraw-Hill, 1986.

Kelly, G. F. "College Males and the New Masculinism." *Sex Information and Education Council of the U.S. (SIECUS) Report,* 1976, *5* (1), 1.

Merton, A. "Father Hunger: The Secret Wound of American Men." *New Age Journal,* 1986, *2* (13), 22.

Nelson, J. B. "Male Sexuality and Masculine Spirituality." *Sex Information and Education Council of the U.S. (SIECUS) Report,* 1985, *13* (4), 1.

Rabinowitz, F., and Cochran, S. "Counseling Men in Groups." In M. Scher, M. Stevens, G. Good, and G. Eichenfield (eds.), *Handbook of Counseling and Psychotherapy with Men.* Newbury Park, Calif.: Sage, 1987.

Spence, J. T., and Helmreich, R. L. "The Attitudes Toward Women Scale." *JSAS Catalog on Selected Documents on Psychology,* 1972, *2,* 66.

Spence, J. T., and Helmreich, R. L. *Masculinity and Femininity: Their Psychological Dimensions, Correlates, and Antecedents.* Austin: University of Texas Press, 1978.

Spence, J. T., Helmreich, R. L., and Stapp, J. "Ratings of Self and Peers on Sex Role Attributes and Their Relation to Self-Esteem and Conceptions of Masculinity and Femininity." *Journal of Personality and Social Psychology,* 1975, *32,* 29–39.

Stein, T. S. "Men's Groups." In K. Solomon and N. B. Levy (eds.), *Men in Transition: Theory and Therapy.* New York: Plenum, 1982.

Fred Leafgren is assistant chancellor for student life at the University of Wisconsin–Stevens Point. He is also one of the founders and codirectors of the National Wellness Institute.

*Counseling center professionals are encouraged to offer
programs and services consistent with male preferences
for seeking help and solving problems.*

Counseling and Psychotherapy with College Men

Beverly Prosser-Gelwick, Kenneth F. Garni

Student affairs professionals are increasingly aware that men are the "at
risk" and "overlooked" population on campus. Because men have
always been the majority population, the bulk of student affairs programming has focused primarily on responding to the perceived needs
of the various underrepresented populations on campuses. Such programs have often overlooked men's unique style of identity formation
and manner of decision making. It is not surprising, therefore, that
many men do not seek help from counseling centers until their problems
are critical. They view the counseling center, if they are aware of its
existence, as a place where they may become even more vulnerable, or a
place where those who can't "handle" their educational problems or
social behavior go in order to maintain their academic status while on
campus.

   Male students are placed at further risk when the institutions in
which they study continue to adhere to traditional societal sex role stereotypes in implementing institutional policies and do not take into consideration the rapidly changing social and economic realities facing men.
The end result is that male students' needs become increasingly hidden
and ignored by those charged with responding to them.

R. J. May and M. Scher (eds.). *Changing Roles for Men on Campus.*
New Directions for Student Services, no. 42. San Francisco: Jossey-Bass, Summer 1988.

Student Use of Counseling Centers

In the face of multiplying stressors on college students, counseling services on campus have become among the primary advocates for student growth and development. As a result, much research has been done in the past three decades on the complex relationship between providers and users of counseling services.

Sex Differences. Perhaps the most consistent findings over time are those related to sex differences in use of counseling services, reports of mental health concerns, and counseling expectations. The prevalence of both mental health concerns and complaints of physical illness have been reported to be lower for men than for women (Kirk, 1973). Men are much less aware of the presence of counseling centers on campus, and they consistently seek counseling help in mental health settings of all types with less frequency than women. Men report significantly fewer psychosocial concerns than women and significantly more concerns with career-related issues. Male clients appear to value more analytically oriented and directive interactions with counselors, while female clients place greater emphasis on and have higher expectations for the facilitative elements inherent in the counseling relationship. Men are more likely to report substance abuse and antisocial personality disorders, whereas women are more likely to report depression, anxiety disorders, and an increased incidence of suicidal behaviors (Koplik and DeVito, 1986). Finally, male clients tend to stay in therapeutic relationships only half as long as female clients (Fabrikant, 1974).

Counselor Preference. A number of studies suggest that male and female clients often select counselors in a manner consistent with the prevailing "positive" view of male mental health. Both male and female clients, when analyzed by problem types, preferred male therapists, ostensibly for their perceived authority, experience, and prestige. On the other hand, students preferred female therapists for their perceived ability to relate to problems of a personal nature (Boulware and Holmes, 1970; Hardin and Yanico, 1983). Johnson (1978) found that counselor gender influenced expected sex roles, with male therapists expected to be "masculine" and their female counterparts expected to provide an androgynous context for the counseling interaction.

Existing research on the relative importance of students' counselor preference on entry into the counseling relationship and expectations concerning counseling outcomes has provided equivocal results. Although much gender preference research indicates that male clients prefer male counselors and would select such a dyad given the choice to do so, a decade of research by Garni (1986) indicates a significant change in the counselor-preference pattern exhibited by male clients over that time. Although there was a higher proportion of female than male clients who sought individual counseling services, significantly higher than their representation in the student population at large, a marked change occurred in counselor selection preference among both male and female clients: There was a significant increase among male clients requesting female therapists and a significant decrease among female clients requesting male therapists. A possible explanation for this change by male clients is the heightened emphasis on the importance of interpersonal relationships and the perceived need for improved social skills among male students as an antidote to expressed feelings of personal isolation and separateness from peers. Concerns with issues of sexual orientation, family systems, and intimacy have also focused more attention on interpersonal interventions on behalf of male clients.

Treatment Preferences. Another change in the use of therapeutic services by college men is reflected in the "length" and "style" of duration of treatment (Garni, 1986). Male clients were significantly less apt to be self-referred than female clients, and males had fewer prior counseling experiences than females. A significantly larger proportion of male clients requested short-term counseling than female clients, although at intake both groups were identified as having similar long-term counseling needs. Male clients sought career and vocational services three times more frequently than women and did not select personal counseling as often as did female clients. Finally, male clients tended to initiate counseling sessions later in the academic year, at times tied to peak academic stress periods (midterms, finals), and later in their academic careers.

Perhaps equally important as counselor selection patterns in planning the allocation and reallocation of available resources to meet changing client demands is the "style" of male clients in accessing counseling relationships. A simple numbers approach to male and female use of services often overlooks more discriminating differences in that use. For example, it is clear from the research previously cited that the majority of male clients come to the counseling relationship later, stay for shorter periods of time, and see counselors less frequently than do the majority of female clients. They involve themselves in sequential counseling relationships, with frequent breaks in their treatment, and with a series of task-focused, seemingly independent interventions throughout their collegiate careers. In addition, it is our experience that male clients also want to make more frequent transfers between counselors and more readily accept changes in the gender of their counselors than do female clients.

Institutional Impact. Clearly, institutional changes affect the frequency and mode of use of available services by potential clients. One result of affirmative action regulations on professional schools, especially in law, engineering, and business programs, has been a sharp increase in female students enrolled in those previously heavily male-dominated programs. The resultant effects on the interactive climate in institutions have had a major impact on the use of available counseling resources. As has been noted, male students tended not to use counseling services. Now, however, their majority status is under challenge, and the resultant feelings of alienation, separation, and fears of failure are brought with increasing frequency to counseling centers.

Male use of counseling services is beginning to reflect changes outside colleges and universities. The consequent pressures and stresses on male students on campus are real and, as such, will certainly be reflected in a change in their interactions with student affairs professionals. Male students need broad, comprehensive assistance in dealing with the myriad pressures inside and outside the classroom. It is essential that counseling centers adjust their own treatment focuses and more actively address the needs of potential male clients. Without such a change in orientation, counseling services run the risk of alienating and overlooking a very large at-risk group.

Male Bonding

The college years are for many men a period of struggle during which authority is challenged, independence is mastered, and the last rites of childhood are played out. "Spend five minutes in a fraternity house," says Nelson (1985), "and you can see how late into life boys still need to be around each other, practicing to be men, sanctioning each other, testing (without admitting it) to see if what they think they think (sic) they know is correct" (p. 48).

Komarovsky (1976) and Pleck (1975) argue that male bonding is not a vehicle for male-male emotional relationships but a substitute for them. On the other hand, Tiger (1969) argued that, for cultural and biological reasons, men are propelled to establish strong ties with other men, thus forming the backbone for social and occupational organizations. If counseling services are to effectively respond to the needs of male students, the conclusions of Komarovsky, Pleck, and Tiger must be integrated into treatment and programming efforts. Whereas many men request counseling from women therapists because they expect that it is easier to self-disclose to women, it may be more appropriate to treat such situations as male-male relationship problems, which are more appropriately treated by focusing on the emotional aspects of male-male interactions. On the other hand, it is not unusual to find male students requesting career and/or academic assistance exclusively from male therapists, when an equally effective, and different, growth experience would be facilitated by a referral to a female therapist. Unless counseling centers can provide comprehensive differential intake procedures that take into account both bonding and self-disclosure needs of male students, male students will continue to be "at risk."

Major Counseling Tasks

Several issues are involved in counseling men: communication, gender role strain, and relationships.

Client-Counselor Communication. One task in counseling is to establish and maintain communication between the client and the therapist and to encourage introspection on the part of the client. Two patterns of communication are discussed by Olsen (1978). The first, instrumental communication, is encouraged and generated by the masculine gender role. The content of the message is of issues and facts to be explained by logic, reasoning, and problem solving. The second, expressive communication, is encouraged and given impetus by the feminine gender role. The content of the message is that relationship is primary. Relationship is developed and sustained by interpersonal skills and messages. The therapist who rejects the assumptions and promises of a patriarchal society and its singular expression of power is in a unique position to help men integrate the two forms of communication. That integration enables men to begin the introspection necessary for personal development. The male therapist able to integrate both patterns for himself generally initiates communication using the instrumental form of interaction, while introducing the expressive as a necessary ingredient to bridge early gender role training and to develop the capacity for complete communication. In contrast, the female therapist may find it more natural to initiate communication at the expressive level, while later integrating the instrumental form of interaction. While Tolson (1977) believes that it will be very difficult for men to "experience the excitement of self-expression and discovery" (p. 19), introspection and feedback made possible by the integration of the two levels of communications can allow men to achieve such goals.

In order for therapists to effectively help male clients integrate the two patterns of communication, they must be alert to, and appreciative of, the predisposition to fall back on socialized modes of communication. For therapists to counter their own internalized perspectives, they must read widely and continue learning about what men and women say about themselves and their relationships to both sexes.

Gender Role Strain. Another task in counseling men is to help relieve the existing gender role strain that results from the discrepancy between the concept of the real self and the ideal self, as described in Chapter One. O'Neil (1981) suggests that anger, hostility, and rage result from the male repression of feminine values, attitudes, and behaviors. When men are able to understand that their fear and hostility is really nonacceptance of self and that they are in fact vulnerable and afraid to give up control, they discover that they must learn to trust themselves, their therapists, and other men and women. The counseling service could be the first safe interpersonal setting that allows men to relax their need to control their emotions and to test out new interpersonal learning.

Developing Relationships. Developing rewarding relationships with others is another task of therapy for men. Men's socialization often prohibits them from relating to women in terms of most women's needs. As men become aware of the "feminine side" of their own nature, they will begin to understand more fully the nature of women's interpersonal, sexual, and emotional needs. Men will also begin to discover the depth of their own needs for sexuality and intimacy. Relationships that consider the needs of both partners generally involve active listening and mutual respect. As a result, men can learn to examine reality as experienced by the partner. They can develop the potential to listen without interrupting, to negotiate without informing, and to accept differences in value systems without threats to self-esteem.

A final task of counseling requires that men examine their relationships with other men. The freedom and courage to enter into friendships with other men will surely be aided by the development of mutually satisfying relationships with women. The development of positive friendships with men will be characterized by acknowledgment of emotions, personal self-disclosures, giving up the need to control self and others, and trust in self and others, without the implication that such characteristics imply either personal inadequacy or homosexuality. Homophobia has often kept men from the joys of same-sex friendships.

What Works with Men

Research over the years has provided much reliable information concerning how men use counseling services. Unless campus psychologists and student affairs professionals use the results of that research, much of which emphasizes how risky entering treatment is perceived to be by the traditional male student, we may make the therapeutic experience ineffective, or inappropriate, for those clients. To avoid doing so, counseling center professionals must fully understand the counseling needs and predispositions of potential male clients as they have been defined by earlier and current research and then—and only then—provide interventions consistent with those expressed needs. Required readings to develop such understanding of male student needs include Good and May (1987), Scher (1981), and Skovholt, Schauble, Gormally, and Davis (1978).

Individual Counseling. At present, males view the requesting and acceptance of help as violating their sense of masculine identity. They take a task-oriented view of counseling, seeking advice and direction given by a counselor in order to control the external environment. In many ways, counseling is entertained as a simple learning experience with a time-limited focus. As long as the male gender identity continues to be threatened by issues of intimacy and interpersonal relatedness, individual therapy will be perceived by male students as unproductive for resolving personal problems (Carlson, 1981).

Chamow (1978) asserted that men enter counseling for three reasons: (1) to "fix" specific problems (for example, drinking, drugs, acting-out problems), (2) when requested to do so by someone else, or (3) when related to the need for marital and/or relationship counseling. As presently offered to male students, individual counseling services often pose far too many risks to maintain the traditional male sex role. Men find it extremely difficult to depend on another person, to express feelings in an honest and genuine manner, and to trust the therapeutic relationship to aid personal growth and development. To be dependent counters the time-honored commitment to independence of thought and action, rationality above all else, and strict adherence to issues of emotional control. As a consequence, male clients tend to disclose less, at least early in the treatment process, with either male or female therapists. It is our view that the manner in which counseling services offer, and evaluate individual treatment interventions often perpetuates the difficulties of self-disclosure for male clients. By promoting adherence to the traditional model of continuous weekly individual sessions through to a completed termination, male "styles" of time of entry into treatment, pacing, duration, and sequencing of therapy, as well as expectations for outcomes, are ignored. To effectively respond to the needs of male clients, counselors must be able to challenge their previous training and experiences regarding the traditional issues of transference and resistance, as well as be willing to redefine operational definitions of both brief and long-term therapies. For example, intake policies might include offering brief interventions and sequential interactions, thereby reducing male clients' potential resistance to long-term therapy.

The foregoing information merely highlights the need to be thoughtful in offering counseling services to male clients. Issues that foster social conflicts for men are often the same issues that make it difficult for them to enter and continue to rely on the individual counseling relationship. Given the narrowed focus of male college students on academic performance and career exploration and development, and the difficulties in interpersonal communications and skills generally attributed to such students, time-limited counseling and task-focused programming addressing men's roles would seem to be a positive, potentially effective strategy for the next decade.

Outreach and Group Programs. Counseling center outreach programming must be developed using the cited research. A program format using a multimedia approach or topic-focused groups lends itself to a process consistent with males' preferred style of interaction and learning. Such programs and groups will provide opportunities for learning through observation, rather than from intrapersonal disclosures, which are often seen by men as exemplifying dependency, weakness, and vulnerability.

While the group holds much promise for new learning for male students, it is equally fraught with potential difficulties that would hamper such learning. As men have considerable difficulty in disclosing personal and sensitive information about themselves to others, much care must go into planning group strategies. Although personal enrichment and growth groups are popular with female clients, they are only successful with a minority of males. On the other hand, groups that allow for focusing personal growth in the larger context of career development and academic success are much more attractive to men. Groups addressing career exploration issues, such as office politics, career mobility, corporate psychology, and management-supervisory skills, frequently allow males to evaluate relationship dynamics in the more restricted, safe framework of vocational concerns. Examples of specific interventions include groups on managing job stress, performance anxiety, building successful careers, executive assessment/potential, eliminating self-defeating behaviors, mini-courses on strategies for academic and vocational success, as well as mentoring programs for students. Further examples of programs designed for college students are listed in the following publications: the *Clearinghouse for Innovative Programs in Mental Health*, Volumes 1 through 5 (1982–1987), the Association of University and College Counseling Center Directors' *Data Bank* (1986), and the *Clearinghouse for Structured Group Programs: Abstracts Catalog* (1985).

In addition, outreach programs that use films, videotapes, and theatrical skits or sketches as a more indirect means of eliciting reactions to issues of socialization and interpersonal relationships seem to have more immediate impact on male participants. Gelwick and Heppner (1981), Wade, Wade, and Croteau (1983), and Morgan, Skovholt, and Orr (1979) have successfully used stimulus films addressing male sex role issues as a means of helping male participants overcome resistance to self-disclosure. Garni (1986) has also reported that presenting a year-long series of films on student life issues (sexuality, sexual abuse, alcoholism, homosexuality, suicide, intimacy, stress management) produced a positive arena for male students to confront feelings about their socialization and to address their need for interpersonal sharing.

Recommended Changes

The view of the "white, middle-class, average-age male college student" as a homogeneous group with similar and traditional needs is now a fallacy. The past fifteen years of the feminist movement and the admission of minority and underprivileged students have radically altered the expectations and needs of traditional male students. In spite of such changes, however, men's basic problem areas have remained remarkably consistent: negative experiences in elementary school, fallout from adolescent male aggressiveness, restrictive emotionality, and believing that vocational success is everything (Skovholt and Hansen, 1980). The clash between traditional and newly emerging cultural expectations supports the definition of today's college men as an "at-risk" population. Faculty, psychologists, and student affairs professionals need to reevaluate their attitudes, expectations, and activities as they educate this frequently overlooked population.

A greater emphasis must be placed on gender-free training of counselors and psychologists that addresses male "styles" as they apply to counseling services usage. We recommend in-service training regarding male student needs, concerns, and developmental issues. More effective use of differential intake procedures and increased flexibility in applying diverse treatment models are equally essential. Further, we urge changes in institutional policies taking into consideration the rapidly changing social and economic realities facing men.

In our opinion, the most important issue is to acknowledge and respect the "style" of male clients. Their initial need is for brief, sequential counseling interventions. Their focus is problem solving. Counseling center brochures and other advertising methods should include identified male needs and themes among appropriate issues for discussion in counseling sessions. These needs encompass educational, vocational, and academic issues. Task-centered counseling allows men to evaluate relationships and personal dynamics under the guise of seeking help with vocational concerns as they relate to choice and identity, relationships and power, politics and advancement, and work and family.

Because men's issues are generally topically focused, they must be met with programming centered on potential solutions rather than on issues of an interpersonal nature. This type of programming allows men to observe and vicariously deal with issues and concerns before committing their emotions and identity needs openly to others. The counseling service also should become much more actively involved with athletic departments, professional schools, and the Greek system. Then, faculty, coaches, and advisers will more readily acknowledge the counseling service as a place that provides counseling and programs for men as they deal with the issues of career, sports, fraternity relationships, and masculinity.

Summary

Traditional methods of counseling, group work, and programming are effective for only a small portion of undergraduate and graduate men

76

on campus. Research shows that men consistently can be differentiated from women in use of counseling services, counselor preference, treatment preferences, and "style" of counseling. Institutional changes resulting from affirmative action have had a dramatic effect on the focus of counseling and programming. This raises the issue of the male population now being overlooked by traditional student services. The issues of male bonding, client-counselor communication, gender role strain, and relationships were discussed with emphasis on what works with men.

It is the responsibility of every student affairs professional to pay heed to the new information in designing and implementing counseling and group interventions as well as outreach programs. Without such attention and commitment, male students will remain increasingly "at risk."

References

Association of University and College Counseling Center Directors. *Data Bank.* College Park: Counseling Center, University of Maryland, 1986.

Boulware, D., and Holmes, D. "Preferences for Therapists and Related Experiences." *Journal of Consulting and Clinical Psychology,* 1970, *35,* 269-277.

Carlson, N. "Male Client-Female Therapist." *Personnel and Guidance Journal,* 1981, *12,* 228-231.

Chamow, L. "Some Thoughts on the Difficulty Men Have Initiating Individual Psychotherapy." *Family Therapy,* 1978, *5,* 67-71.

Clearinghouse for Innovative Programs in Mental Health. Vols. 1-5. Austin: Counseling-Psychological Services Center, University of Texas, 1982-1987.

Clearinghouse for Structured Group Programs: Abstracts Catalog. Austin: Counseling-Psychological Services Center, University of Texas, 1985.

Fabrikant, B. "The Psychotherapist and the Female Patient: Perceptions, Misconceptions, and Change." In V. Franks and V. Burtle (eds.), *Women in Therapy.* New York: Brunner/Mazel, 1974.

Garni, K. *Annual Report.* Boston: Counseling Center, Suffolk University, 1986.

Gelwick, B. P., and Heppner, P. P. "Men's Lives: Toward a Proactive Sex Role Intervention for Men and Women." *Journal of College Student Personnel,* 1981, *22,* 559-560.

Good, G., and May, R. J. "Developmental Issues, Environmental Influences, and the Nature of Therapy with College Men." In M. Scher, M. Stevens, G. Good, and G. Eichenfield (eds.), *Handbook of Counseling and Psychotherapy with Men.* Newbury Park, Calif.: Sage, 1987.

Hardin, S., and Yanico, B. "Counseling Gender, Type of Problem, and Expectations About Counseling." *Journal of Counseling Psychology,* 1983, *30* (2), 294-297.

Johnson, D. "Students' Sex Preferences and Sex Role Expectations for Counselors." *Journal of Counseling Psychology,* 1978, *25,* 557-562.

Kirk, B. A. "Characteristics of Users of Counseling Centers and Psychiatric Services on a College Campus." *Journal of Counseling Psychology,* 1973, *20* (5), 463-470.

Komarovsky, M. *Dilemmas of Masculinity: A Study of College Youth.* New York: Norton, 1976.

Koplik, E., and DeVito, A. "Problems of Freshmen: Comparison of Classes of 1976 and 1986." *Journal of College Student Personnel,* 1986, *3,* 124-131.

Morgan, J., Skovholt, T., and Orr, J. "Career Counseling with Men: The Shifting Focus." In S. G. Weinroch (ed.), *Career Counseling: Theoretical and Practical Perspectives.* New York: McGraw-Hill, 1979.

Nelson, P. "On Differences: One Man's View of Men and Their Bodies." *Ms.,* 1985, *14* (3), 48-114.

Olsen, K. *Hey Man, Open Up and Live.* New York: Fawcett Gold Medal, 1978.

O'Neil, J. "Gender Role Conflict and Strain in Men's Lives. Implications for Psychiatrists, Psychologists, and Other Human Service Providers." In K. Solomon and N. B. Levy (eds.), *Men in Transition: Changing Male Roles, Theory, and Therapy.* New York: Plenum Press, 1981.

Pleck, J. "Masculinity-Femininity: Current and Alternative Paradigms." *Sex Roles,* 1975, *1,* 161-178.

Scher, M. (ed.). "Counseling Males." *Personnel and Guidance Journal,* 1981, *60* (4) (special issue).

Skovholt, T., and Hansen, A. "Men's Development: A Prospective and Some Themes." In T. Skovholt, P. Schauble, and R. Davis (eds.), *Counseling Men.* Monterey, Calif.: Brooks/Cole, 1980.

Skovholt, T., Schauble, P., Gormally, J., and Davis, R. (eds.). "Counseling Men." *Counseling Psychologist,* 1978, *7* (4) (special issue).

Tiger, L. *Men in Groups.* New York: Random House, 1969.

Tolson, A. *The Limits of Masculinity: Male Identity and Women's Liberation.* New York: Harper & Row, 1977.

Wade, L., Wade, J., and Croteau, J. "The Man and the Male: A Creative Outreach Program on Men's Roles." *Journal of College Student Personnel,* 1983, *9,* 460-461.

Beverly Prosser-Gelwick is director of the Counseling and Testing Service at the University of New Hampshire.
Kenneth F. Garni is the director of the Counseling Center at Suffolk University. Both authors are past presidents of the International Association of Counseling Services and former members of the board of directors of the Association of University and College Counseling Centers.

Changing roles present new dilemmas, challenges, and
possibilities for the male student services professional.

Men and Leadership in College Student Personnel Services

Jon C. Dalton

Leadership in college student personnel services roles has traditionally been conceived in terms of male roles and masculine qualities. The earliest colleges in America were restricted to young men, and for over two centuries colleges educated young men almost exclusively. It was well into the twentieth century before women composed more than one-quarter of the enrollment in the nation's colleges (Rudolph, 1977). This historical male orientation in higher education shaped student affairs leadership roles and in some respects left a negative legacy for men and women professionals today. In this chapter we shall examine some of the ways in which history, social attitudes, job expectations, and sex roles influence men in student affairs leadership roles.

Two points should be noted at the outset. First, the focus of concern in this chapter is on men and the problems they confront in student affairs leadership roles. This does not suggest that these problems are unique to males. The chapter is written from a male perspective in order to focus on issues with which men struggle in leadership roles. Second, the chapter is written from my personal perspective and observations as a student affairs practitioner and leader. I believe such an approach can be

R. J. May and M. Scher (eds.). *Changing Roles for Men on Campus.*
New Directions for Student Services, no. 42. San Francisco: Jossey-Bass, Summer 1988.

valuable in discussing changing roles of men in higher education and in providing insights into how some male leaders perceive and cope with leadership and masculinity.

Masculine Bias in Student Affairs History

The earliest student affairs deans were men chosen from the faculty to monitor student conduct and to discipline students (Rudolph, 1977). Even after women began to enroll in college, men were usually selected for student affairs leadership roles because discipline of the young was customarily regarded by society as a male role.

The earliest deans of students were typically strong male role models chosen on the basis of their ability to guide and admonish their student charges. They were chosen from among the faculty primarily because they were regarded as strong ethical role models. When LeBaron Russell Briggs was appointed dean at Harvard in 1890, his primary role was to monitor students' conduct and promote in them good manners, honesty, a sense of fairness, and respect for authority (Brown, 1926). In addition to their responsibility for the discipline of students, the early deans were charged with the moral or character education of students. They were expected to model the values promoted by the institution as well as instill those values among the students.

This early responsibility of male deans for the discipline and moral development of young men no doubt helped create a legacy of male orientation in leadership roles. Later, the evolution of in loco parentis as a formal legal responsibility of colleges in the twentieth century served to strengthen the patriarchal character of student affairs leadership roles. Colleges were expected to monitor the welfare and safety of students placed in their charge. In the first half of the twentieth century, men and women deans had almost complete authority to monitor students' behavior and to summarily discipline students for inappropriate personal conduct. With the demise of in loco parentis and the movement of colleges and universities away from parental control of student conduct, the focus of student affairs work shifted to issues of education and student development.

Although the early male orientation of student affairs roles has been radically transformed, there continues to be some bias toward masculine characteristics and role expectations in senior leadership positions. This bias is linked not so much to the authority and power of deans over the conduct of students, although this role continues to be far more important than acknowledged in the literature, but to deans' authority and power in institutional resource and policy decisions. I shall examine some of the forms of this bias in the sections to follow. The male bias in student affairs leadership roles is ultimately not only detrimental to women but it also carries some confining masculine stereotypes that adversely affect men.

Perceptions of Student Affairs Leaders

A variety of social perceptions and expectations reinforce the male role orientation in student affairs leadership positions. Rickard (1985) claims that there are deeply rooted social forces, including myths and biases, that influence perceptions and decisions about men and women in leadership roles. In my experience, when student affairs staff are asked to rate the most important duties to be performed by the chief student affairs leaders, they generally rank as a top priority the ability to defend and protect employees' rights and resources.

Next on the hierarchy of perceived leadership requirements is the priority of enhancing individual and collective influence within the institution. The first priority concerns protection of territory; the second involves the expansion of influence within the larger organization. In order to fulfill these expectations, a student affairs leader is expected to be able to acquire and execute power. Because maleness has traditionally been associated with political as well as physical prowess, the perception is often held that men are somehow better able to acquire and wield power more effectively than women (Stearns, 1979).

This male bias also contributes to the perception that effective student affairs leaders must be assertive, if not aggressive, in order to protect and enhance the interests of employees. Since males are more intentionally socialized to be aggressive, they may be viewed as better able to handle leadership roles, which frequently call for assertive and even combative behavior. Allen (1984) argues that women in leadership roles will routinely encounter doubts from others regarding their ability to take charge and get tough. In search activities for vice-presidents and deans of students, interviewers are especially interested in how tough a candidate is, how she or he will perform under pressure, and how strong the individual will be in representing and defending the interests of the organization. Women may often have to prove a higher degree of competence than men in order to dispel prejudicial attitudes about their lack of aggressiveness and difficulty in asserting power. Since student affairs is widely regarded as the least powerful of the major administrative units in the college or university organization, staff may be especially concerned that leaders are strong advocates and forceful leaders.

Student affairs leaders are also expected to be able to motivate and inspire loyalty in followers and maintain a sense of order and stability throughout the organization. These leadership qualities are often attributed to males because the qualities of strength, order, stability, and loyalty are associated with strong advocacy leadership styles. The underrepresentation of women role models in senior student affairs positions serves to perpetuate the bias that men are somehow better suited for such leadership roles.

The implications of a male bias in leadership roles creates problems for both women and men. The problems created for women are more obvious. Women encounter barriers of attitudes and perceptions that make it more difficult for them to be fully appreciated for their leadership skills and experience. They find that they must demonstrate competencies taken for granted in their male peers. Moreover, they are frequently held to more rigorous standards of review and performance than men, which makes success as a leader more difficult to achieve.

The problems created for men in leadership roles are less overt but nonetheless real. Men are expected to fulfill stereotypical masculine role obligations of leadership: to be aggressive, dominant, tough under pressure, an enforcer of order and stability, and an agent of power and influence. Fulfilling such expectations of masculinity can make it difficult for men to display vulnerability, to express caring and nurturance in relationships, and to admit uncertainty and need for assistance. Moreover, Gilligan (1982) believes that men develop less fully in the areas of empathy, caring, and nurturance because they have been socialized to view these attributes as less important. Delworth and Seeman (1984) make much the same point in arguing that men's development centers on issues of autonomy and only later on issues of relationship and intimacy.

When men in student affairs leadership positions are unable or deterred from caring, nurturing roles, they may find that they become isolated, unable to share their problems openly with others or to solicit help because of the fear that such behavior will be viewed as a sign of weakness. Research by Stearns (1979) and O'Neil (1981) indicates that too much stress on masculinity can distort men's nature. It puts men out of touch with their emotions so that they are too silent, too aggressive, too achievement-oriented, and unable to form real friendships.

If they are limited in their opportunities to express these needs, men may, over time, find leadership roles to be unsatisfying and even dehumanizing. The higher the level of leadership responsibility, the greater are the pressures to fulfill the stereotypical masculine role expectations. It is lonely at the top for men and women, but for different reasons. Women are judged by excessive standards of performance and isolated by their underrepresentation; men may feel inner isolation because they have few support networks and feel they cannot risk vulnerability in their exercise of power. While the socialization of men prepares them for a certain degree of isolation and individualism, it does not meet the need of men in leadership roles for a supportive network of friendships and collegial relationships. Men in leadership roles not only must struggle with dehumanizing, unrealistic role expectations but they may also lack the skills to promote and sustain a network of human relationships to prevent their isolation. The most effective leaders are those who are able to express both authority and caring. To be a leader who conveys concern and caring for others, one must be able to build a network of interdependent relationships.

Recruitment and Professional Development of Men

Data on entering college freshmen suggest that men are more success-oriented and materialistic than women (Astin, 1986). They place greater importance upon achieving status in life and see career mobility as one of the most important measures of personal success. Men carry this high achievement and professional mobility orientation into their work in student affairs roles. Young men entering student affairs positions are especially concerned about career mobility and how to move up quickly to higher levels of professional responsibility and status. Because of traditional social pressures on them, they are inclined to base their self-esteem on their economic worth (Cooper and Robinson, 1987).

The institutional environment in higher education may contribute to the male bias in leadership roles by rewarding masculine models of leadership. Leaders who are strong, autonomous, and role-oriented are viewed more favorably than leaders whose behavior is primarily other-directed, empathetic, and concerned with relationships (Delworth and Seeman, 1984).

Because of their high achievement orientation, men are often more unwilling than women to invest significant time and energy in networking relationships, especially if they do not consider these investments highly relevant to the attainment of specific professional goals. In such situations, the tendency to focus on tangible reward and achievement may serve to inhibit men from developing supportive relationships that help them avoid social and professional isolation.

The college student services professional is a career field that does not generally provide high status and material rewards compared to many other professions. The number of men entering the field has declined steadily over the past two decades, primarily because the profession does not appear to offer sufficient professional advancement opportunities and material rewards.

Recruiting men for student affairs positions requires special attention to status issues because of their concern for career mobility. Men are especially concerned about job titles and job advancement opportunities. Starting salary is very important but may often be less important than job title and job advancement potential, since salary can be viewed as temporary.

Because of their high status needs, men are often dependent upon regular, tangible recognition of their career progress in order to maintain a high level of motivation and achievement. When job advancement opportunities are not available, salary becomes the most tangible symbol of status and success. Without regular, objective confirmation of achievement, men are likely to feel a loss of self-esteem and begin to question their competencies. This is especially so of new professionals who generally need more outward confirmation of achievement because they lack the self-assurance that comes with practical experience. It is a difficult aspect of professional life for men in student affairs roles to adjust to the fact that career advancement opportunities generally lag far behind career aspirations. Men with a high need for rapid success and achievement may leave the profession, change jobs, or become resigned to failure (Holmes, Verrier, and Chisholm, 1983).

One of the most valuable staff development experiences for young men is the opportunity to share with their supervisor and with male and female peers their career aspirations and attitudes about job success and achievement. In such situations, young men learn to recognize that some of the most rewarding accomplishments of work are personal and intrinsic, and cannot be measured by title or compensation. Effective mentoring by a supervisor can also help young men achieve a broader viewpoint on the meaning of success in professional roles.

Men's support groups can also provide an important resource to assist men to be more direct and open in expressing feelings and to convey caring in interpersonal relationships. Cochran and Rabinowitz (1983) feel that an important role of such groups is to enable men to move beyond intellectualizing and debating their concerns and learn how to convey feelings more openly.

Although it is not unique to student affairs roles, one of the difficulties for men in leadership roles is balancing a high personal achievement orientation with the altruistic roles and values of a helping profession. Pursuing personal status and recognition in a profession whose primary roles are service-oriented can result in a serious clash of values. How does one balance a personal need for recognition and achievement with a commitment to serve the needs of students? Men have particular problems with this professional ethical dilemma; they are expected to place the needs of students primary in their professional roles, but they are not socialized to be highly motivated toward caring and nurturing roles.

Moreover, time and effort spent on direct service-related activities may not serve to enhance those skills or credentials that most directly promote professional advancement. Men of conscience forever struggle with this dichotomy in their work, especially when they are new in the field. They are not likely to remain in the profession long unless they resolve in a satisfactory way the inherent tension between self and others.

When the tension is resolved too greatly in the direction of self, it can result in estrangement. When it is resolved too much in the direction of others, a loss of motivation can result.

Networking and Socializing on the Job

Because of their greater orientation toward competition and concern for status, it may be more difficult for men to develop and sustain close interpersonal relationships than women. When men socialize on the job, they are likely to talk about work-related issues or casual social topics, such as sports or recreational activities. They typically avoid talking about feelings, personal problems, values, and beliefs. Consequently, relationships among men on the job tend to be business-oriented, casual, and impersonal. Men generally do not open up sufficiently on a personal level to develop close interpersonal relationships with other men with whom they work.

Relationships among men are likely to be based on perceptions of status and power rather than on mutual experiences of trust and shared values. Networking among men is important but too often functions more for the purpose of enhancing one's own influence and status than for personal support or feedback. Pancrazio and Gray (1982) describe male networking as a system for professional support highly dependent on favors, promises, and connections with people of influence. One of the important roles a men's support group can play in a student affairs organization is to recognize men's networking needs and to provide structured opportunities for it to occur.

Too often men are hesitant to share feelings and problems with other men because of their fear of intimacy, especially if such behavior may be mistaken for homosexual interests. Display of affection can be difficult between men because such behavior does not readily fit the assertive, competitive male role image. Consequently, men might have trouble experiencing close personal friendships in work relationships with other men. This is especially so for men in leadership positions because leaders' interactions with others are greatly influenced by authority relationships.

The fear of having personal intimacy mistaken for a homosexual advance or inclination deters many men from disclosing their feelings to other men (Miller, 1983). Unless there is a high degree of trust, some men fear that intimate disclosures could be misinterpreted as signs of personal weakness or sexual overtures. In addition to avoiding intimacy with other men, some men exaggerate stereotypical male characteristics as a way of certifying their maleness. Such homophobic behavior creates problems in the work setting because many men and women are repelled by "macho" behavior. Rather than conveying strength and sex role definition, homophobic behavior conveys insecurity and insensitivity that can greatly diminish leadership effectiveness.

Widespread fear of being seen as homosexual restrains expressions of caring and intimacy between men and creates a social distance that can make close friendship with other males very difficult. Such fear may isolate men in narrowly defined social roles and inhibit them from learning from others who share common experiences.

Sex Role Issues in Student Affairs Administration

Sex role stereotypes and taboos also serve as hindrances to the expression of affection and intimacy by males in work-related situations. If most men avoid appearances of intimacy with other men because of fear of being labeled homosexual, they are not so constrained when it comes to relationships with women. On the contrary, men often feel that sexually assertive behavior is expected in their relationships with the opposite sex. Such behavior, it is often believed, is not only socially approved but even confirming of one's maleness. When such attitudes are combined with authority in the job setting, problems of sexual harassment may result. When men view women as objects of sexual advance, feel sexually assertive behavior is expected and legitimated, and have the power to reward and/or punish the individual who is the object of their behavior, some very dehumanizing activities can occur within the work place.

Sexual harassment in its most overt forms involves physical as well as psychological intimidation. Demeaning treatment that men would not condone in other relationships is regarded as somehow permissible in the work setting because of deeply held stereotypical views about sex roles. While physical harassment and threat are often problems, psychological intimidation may be the most insidious aspect of sexual harassment.

Fear of accusation of sexual harassment may cause men to take special precautions to avoid any appearance of sexual innuendo. The interactions of men with women may appear to become more formal and less sympathetic because of the deliberate avoidance of behaviors and expressions of affection. The constraining of men's interactions with women in the work setting can create more social distance in their interpersonal relationships. Because many men perceive they can more freely joke, touch, and express frank opinions with other men, they are likely to feel closer to them because of the greater openness in their relationships. The spontaneity and openness of men's interactions with each other is not unnoticed by women who are likely to interpret such behavior as gender bias or even personal rejection. It is particularly important for male leaders not to allow sexual taboos to negatively affect their interactions and communications with women staff. To do so not only has obvious negative repercussions for women but it can desensitize men and make them less effective as leaders by narrowing their range of communications and interactions.

One of the most important tasks of leadership in student affairs is fostering a positive sense of community among staff. To experience a sense of community one must feel included, supported, and, to some extent, understood. Where there is a strong sense of community in an organization, individuals are more likely to take risks, participate, and develop pride and loyalty to the organization. Fostering community in student affairs organizations requires, more than anything else, effective communication skills and the ability to convey concern and caring. Some staff are content with merely a sense of order and stability in the work environment; most, however, want a sense of community and judge a leader by his or her ability to promote it in the organization.

Men often have difficulty promoting community in organizations because of their inclination to rely on power and authority to organize and define staff roles and expectations. Men leaders often seem surprised to find that although the use of authority can achieve compliance in groups, it seldom creates loyalty or a sense of community. Men who have developed the skills to listen and empathize and to express concern and affection are better able to model the kind of behavior that creates and sustains community in an organization.

One of the difficulties men sometimes encounter in leadership roles is the lack of affection for them by their staff. Men often avoid outright expressions of affection and are inclined to assume that they are well liked if their staff simply show outward respect toward them and conformity to their leadership. Men may confuse compliance with respect and confuse respect with affection. It is usually surprising and sometimes even devastating for men to learn that they are perceived as cold and uncaring individuals.

Because they are socialized to tolerate situations without complaint and generally have weak support networks, men may naively believe that others understand the lonely ordeal of leadership and comprehend the silence of leaders. It is painful for men to learn that coworkers may have little empathy and understanding of leadership problems. If coworkers do not experience openness and affection in their interactions with a male leader, they will conclude that he is, at best, not a very perceptive person and, at worst, an uncaring individual.

Conclusion

The challenges of leadership for men in student affairs roles reflect the dilemmas of men's opposing characteristics: how to be stern and yet forgiving, tough and also gentle, strong without losing a sense of vulnerability. Men in leadership roles must struggle with the inner tension of these opposing emotional forces and their conflicting role demands. There is today a new prospect for androgyny, a change in the male character that may help men to achieve a more natural balance between these forces and reduce the inner tension produced by confining sex roles. Such androgyny can have important implications for the work environment. It can help liberate men from the emotional bondage of a confining role stereotype as well as humanize their leadership style and interactions with others.

Ultimately a new sense of manhood is needed, based upon concepts and behaviors that reflect fewer gender distinctions and more humane values. Men can help promote this new sense of manhood through their efforts to examine male roles and men's issues in college student affairs.

References

Allen, L. H. "On Being a Vice President for Academic Affairs." *Journal of the National Association of Women Deans, Administrators, and Counselors,* 1984, *47* (4), 8-15.

Astin, A. *The American Freshman: National Norms for Fall 1986.* Cooperative Institutional Research Program. Los Angeles: University of California, 1986.

Brown, R. W. *Dean Briggs.* New York: Harper & Row, 1926.

Cochran, S. V., and Rabinowitz, F. E. "An Experimental Men's Group for the University Community." *Journal of College Student Personnel,* 1983, *24* (2), 163-164.

Cooper, S. E., and Robinson, D.A.G. "A Comparison of Career, Home and Leisure Values of Male and Female Students in Engineering and the Sciences." *Journal of College Student Personnel,* 1987, *28* (1), 66-70.

Delworth, U., and Seeman, D. "The Ethics of Care: Implications of Gilligan for the Student Personnel Profession." *Journal of College Student Personnel,* 1984, *25* (6), 489-492.

Gilligan, C. *In a Different Voice.* Cambridge, Mass.: Harvard University Press, 1982.

Holmes, D., Verrier, D., and Chisholm, P. "Persistence in Student Affairs Work: Attitudes and Job Shifts Among Master's Program Graduates." *Journal of College Student Personnel,* 1983, *24* (5), 438-442.

Miller, S. *Men and Friendship.* Boston: Houghton Mifflin, 1983.

O'Neil, J. M. "Patterns of Gender Role Conflict and Strain: The Fear of Femininity in Men's Lives." *Personnel and Guidance Journal,* 1981, *60,* 203-210.

Pancrazio, S. B., and Gray, R. G. "Networking for Professional Women: A Collegial Model." *Journal of the National Association of Women Deans, Administrators, and Counselors,* 1982, *45* (3), 16-19.

Rickard, S. T. "The Achievement of Student Affairs Officers: Progress Toward Equity." *Journal of College Student Personnel,* 1985, *26* (1), 5-10.

Rudolph, F. *Curriculum: A History of the American Undergraduate Course of Study Since 1636.* San Francisco: Jossey-Bass, 1977.

Stearns, P. N. *Be a Man! Males in Modern Society.* New York: Holmes and Meier, 1979.

Jon C. Dalton is vice-president for student affairs at Northern Illinois University. He has published numerous articles on value issues in college student personnel work, including the monograph Promoting Values Education in Student Development.

*Selected readings, program resources, and organizations for
promoting new roles for men are described.*

Resources for Promoting Change in Men's Lives

Ronald J. May

Through the mid 1970s, publications examining the male role were virtually nonexistent in both the popular and professional literature. Then
several books appeared in the popular press that critically examined the
effects of male socialization (see the section that follows on conciousness
raising books). Though now somewhat dated, these self-help books are
still quite useful for creating an awareness of men's issues.

Later, academicians and practicing professionals began to address
the male role in professional publications (see the sections on counseling
interventions and male development). Authors began to present developmental theories and research to more fully understand transition roles for
men. Solomon and Levy (1982) might be considered to be the first "psychology of men" text. Such publications enable professionals to move
beyond traditional beliefs in conceptualizing and responding to the current needs of men.

Developing innovative interventions requires resources and support. Numerous films, videotapes, and record albums have been produced
in recent years that vividly portray the pain, confusion, and humor that
men experience in struggling with changing roles. Several national men's
organizations have evolved to provide opportunities to receive emotional
support, share ideas and resources, and organize political action efforts.

R. J. May and M. Scher (eds.). *Changing Roles for Men on Campus.*
New Directions for Student Services, no. 42. San Francisco: Jossey-Bass, Summer 1988.

These groups typically hold annual meetings, organize resource networks, and publish newsletters.

Books: Counseling Interventions

Scher, M. (ed.). "Counseling Males." *Personnel and Guidance Journal* (currently titled *Journal for Counseling and Development*), 1981, *60* (4) (special issue).

A call for counselors to address the changing needs of men. Individual chapters on gays, teenage fathers, uncoupling, career development, men's violence, men's groups, bodywork, and counselor training.

Scher, M., Stevens, M., Good, G., and Eichenfield, G. (eds.). *Handbook of Counseling and Psychotherapy with Men.* Newbury Park, Calif.: Sage, 1987.

A comprehensive text of the most recent developments in therapeutic interventions for men. Chapter topics emphasize key counseling issues and working with special groups of men.

Skovholt, T., Schauble, P., Gormally, J., and Davis, R. (eds.). "Counseling Men." *Counseling Psychologist*, 1978, *7* (4) (special issue).

A collection of articles by counseling psychologists addressing men's issues. Chapters include discussions of developmental transitions, sexuality, fathering, counseling process, and a number of specific intervention programs.

Books: Consciousness-Raising

The following books critically examine the traditional male role, outline the negative effects of male socialization, and encourage greater role flexibility and emotional expression. Typically they cover such topics as work roles, sexuality, fathering, homophobia, and male friendships.

David, D. S., and Brannon, R. *The Forty-Nine Percent Majority: The Male Sex Role.* Reading, Mass.: Addison-Wesley, 1976.
Farrell, W. *The Liberated Man.* New York: Bantam Books, 1975.
Garfinkel, P. *In a Man's World.* New York: Mentor, 1985.
Goldberg, H. *The Hazards of Being Male.* New York: Signet, 1976.
Goldberg, H. *The New Male.* New York: Morrow, 1979.
Pleck, J. H., and Sawyer, J. (eds.). *Men and Masculinity.* Englewood Cliffs, N.J.: Prentice-Hall, 1974.

Books: Fathers and Sons

Kafka, F. *Letter to His Father.* New York: Schocken, 1966.
A classic piece of literature by the German existentialist, Franz

Kafka. Kafka writes the letter to his father eloquently expressing the pain, frustration, and despair of their estranged relationship.

Osherson, S. *Finding Our Fathers.* New York: Free Press, 1986.

This book relates struggles in male development to unfinished business in relationships with fathers. Osherman's personal disclosures demonstrate how the reemergence of these issues in current roles as a lover or father provide opportunities for healing the wounds between father and son.

Books: Male Development

Gilligan, C. *In a Different Voice.* Cambridge, Mass.: Harvard University Press, 1982.

A landmark book outlining new perspectives on developmental differences between males and females. Although based on moral reasoning research, Gilligan addresses profound stylistic differences in perception and values.

Levinson, D. J. *The Seasons of a Man's Life.* New York: Knopf, 1978.

A comprehensive theory of adult male development based on the longitudinal study of forty Harvard graduates. Levinson postulates predictable life stages and transitions that serve to develop a core life structure.

Rubin, L. *Intimate Strangers.* New York: Harper & Row, 1983.

An examination of gender role changes for men and women and the implications for intimate male-female relationships.

Solomon, K., and Levy, N. B. *Men in Transition.* New York: Plenum, 1982.

A collection of theory and research-based chapters on male development, needs of special populations, and therapeutic interventions. One of the first comprehensive texts to address the psychology of men.

Books: Other Annotated Bibliographies

August, E. R. *Men's Studies.* Littleton, Colo.: Libraries Unlimited, 1985.

An annotated bibliography of almost 600 pieces of men's literature. This interdisciplinary collection covers a wide variety of topics related to men's issues.

American Association for Counseling and Development, Committee on Men. *Men's Issues: A Bibliography.* Alexandria, Va.: American Association for Counseling and Development, 1987.

A comprehensive listing of men's books, journal articles, and periodicals relevant to the student services practitioner. This bibliography is organized by topical categories and is updated on a regular basis.

Media Resources

Films

Arlyck, R. *An Acquired Taste.* 16mm, 26 min. 1982. Distributed by New Day Films, 22 Riverview Dr., Wayne, N.J. 07470-3191. (201) 633-0212.

As this filmmaker turns forty, Ralph Arlyck reviews the school, work, and media images that have shaped his life as a man. The film poses critical questions about the pursuit of success.

Auburn University Rape Awareness Committee (B. Burkhart, chair). *It Still Hurts.* 24 min. 1984. Distributed by Campus Crime Prevention Programs, P. O. Box 204, Goshen, Ky. 40026. (502) 228-1499.

This potent film includes a portrayal of a typical campus date rape and an interview with an actual victim of acquaintance rape. The classic identifying symptoms and rape trauma process are portrayed.

Hanig, J., and Roberts, W. *Men's Lives.* 16mm, 43 min. Distributed by New Day Films, 22 Riverview Dr., Wayne, N.J. 07470-3191. (201) 633-0212.

This Academy Award-winning documentary examines the contributing influences to the male mystique. Two men interview their high school teachers, reflect on their childhood heroes, and speak frankly with men and boys about their images of masculinity.

Rasmussen, L., and Heriza, T., with Garrison, A. *Heroes and Strangers.* 16mm, 29 min. Distributed by New Day Films, 22 Riverview Dr., Wayne, N.J. 07470-3191. (201) 633-0212.

Two young adults, a man and a woman, return home to attempt to break through the silence in their relationships with their fathers. Their interaction reveals the complex social and economic forces affecting the role of fathers.

Records

Morgan, G. "At the Edge." Flying Fish, 1304 W. Schubert St., Chicago, Ill. 60614. (312) 528-5455.

Morgan, G. "Finally Letting It Go." Flying Fish, 1304 W. Schubert St., Chicago, Ill. 60614. (312) 528-5455.

Morgan, G. "It Comes with the Plumbing." Nexus, P. O. Box 4082, Bellingham, Wa. 98227. (206) 647-0766.

Geof Morgan's folk music provides tender, passionate, and humorous portrayals of men's issues. His lyrics' themes include power and competition, sexuality, homophobia, and men's violence.

Organizations and Publications

Committee on Men, American Association for Counseling and Development (AACD). UW YWCA Community Center, 306 N. Brooks, Madison, Wisc. 53715. (608) 257-2534.

A committee of AACD men appointed to promote convention programs and distribute information and resources on men's issues.

National Organization of Changing Men (NOCM). P. O. Box 93, Charleston, Ill. 61920-0093. (815) 432-3010.

A profeminist, gay affirmative organization promoting changing roles for men. Publishes a regular newsletter, *Brother.* Sponsors an annual Men and Masculinity Conference offering programs on personal development and political action.

Nurturing News. Nurturing Press, 187 Caselli Ave., San Francisco, Calif. 94114. (415) 861-0847.

Standing Committee for Men, American College Personnel Association (Fred Leafgren, membership chair). Division of Student Life, Delzell Hall, University of Wisconsin–Stevens Point, Stevens Point, Wisc. 54481. (715) 346-2611.

The Standing Committee advocates the changing needs of male college students and male student service professionals. Activities include sponsoring convention programs, encouraging supportive relationships between men in ACPA, mentoring young professionals, and providing networks for sharing program resources and research.

Ronald J. May is the director of the University Counseling Center at the University of Oregon. He currently chairs the Standing Committee for Men of the American College Personnel Association. Over the past decade, he has worked with men's issues as an author, researcher, educator, and psychotherapist.

Major themes presented in each chapter are summarized.

Concluding Remarks

Ronald J. May, Murray Scher

College students today are living at the dawn of a new day with respect to their roles as men and women. Some are only vaguely aware of the change that is occurring, while others clearly see the possibilities and are actively involved in changing their lives.

Wherever these students may live on the continuum of gender role consciousness, their principal hope for finding guidance and support may lie with student services professionals. The contributors to this sourcebook have attempted to clarify issues and stimulate ideas for meeting the challenges of this changing consciousness.

Several themes arose as the various authors addressed the issues. First, men and women clearly differ in their styles of perceiving the world, processing information, and relating to others. May summarized the differences noted by developmental theorists. Eichenfield observed how the differences vary further among subpopulations of men. Prosser-Gelwick and Garni discussed how the different styles effect help-seeking behavior. As helping professionals, we must present our messages and interventions in a voice that can be heard by male students.

Second, we must be patient and set realistic expectations for changing men. Dalton outlined the long history of traditional male roles in higher education. Scher, Canon, and Stevens discussed the complex interactions between male students and their college environments. Too often we expect men to make changes without appreciating the change process.

R. J. May and M. Scher (eds.). *Changing Roles for Men on Campus.*
New Directions for Student Services, no. 42. San Francisco: Jossey-Bass, Summer 1988.

We promote change more effectively when we recognize current strengths and gently encourage movement into new territory.

Finally, May and Dalton emphasized the importance of changing campus environments to promote new roles for male students. We must realize we have been acculturated in a sexist society. We all express this sexism in our professional roles, though it may be subtle and unconscious. Rather than deny our sexism, we must acknowledge it and demonstrate to students pathways for overcoming it. Within our campus environments, we must confront the sexism inherent in our policies and programs. We need to create a campus culture that welcomes and rewards, rather than punishes, gender role change.

Ronald J. May is the director of the University Counseling Center at the University of Oregon. He currently chairs the Standing Committee for Men of the American College Personnel Association. Over the past decade, he has worked with men's issues as an author, researcher, educator, and psychotherapist.

Murray Scher is in the independent practice of psychotherapy in Greeneville, Tennessee. A founder and former chair of the Standing Committee for Men of the American College Personnel Association, he has written on gender role issues or men.

Index

A

Academic courses, in programs for men, 62–63

Acceptance, levels in college men, 54

Acquaintance rape: on college campuses, 10; and fraternity men, 43; and gender role strain, 24–25; resources for examination of, 94

Adult male students, 46–47; characteristics of, 46; in dual-career relationships, 46–47; and gender role strain, 46–47; interventions with, 47

Adult men, and development of gender identity, 12–13

African students, stereotypes of, 39

Against All Odds, as marketing tool for men's programs, 63

AIDS: concerns over testing for, 39; crisis, 37–38; as issue in programs for men, 31; as issue in workshops, 60

Alcohol: as factor in rape, 25; as issue in programs for men, 31

Allen, L. H., 81, 88

Amatea, E., 47, 49

American Association for Counseling and Development (AACD), 32–33, 58, 93–94, 95

American College Personnel Association (ACPA), 32, 95

An Acquired Taste, 59

Anderson, T. R., 40, 49

Androgyny: assessment for, 56; and role models, 7; theoretical basis of, 6

Animal House, and stereotyping fraternity men, 43

Arlyck, R., 64, 94

Assessment, 55–57; instruments for, 56–57; and value to individual, 56

Association of University and College Counseling Center Directors, 27, 74, 76

Astin, A., 83, 88

Athletes (male), 40–42; and gender role strain, 41; insulation of, 41, 42; interventions for, 41–42; needs of, 41; stereotypes of 40–41

Attitudes Toward Women Scale, 57

Auburn University Rape Awareness Committee, 94

August, E. R., 93

Awareness, levels in college men, 53–54

B

Banning, J. H., 14, 16

Baron, A., 36, 51

Barr, M. J., 22, 34

Bausch-Altman, E., 42, 49

Bem Sex Role Inventory, 56

Bem, S. L., 56, 64

Berzins, J., 57, 64

Bias: male, in student services leadership, 80–81, 82; in research, 11

Bisexual men, 37–39; and AIDS crisis, 37–38, 39; counseling needs of, 38; in fraternities, 44; interventions with, 38–39

Blann, F. W., 40–41, 49

Blimling, G. S., 45, 49

Blocher, D. H., 14, 16

Boles, J., 6, 16, 56, 64

Bonding, 9, 70

"Bookends," 58–59

"Born Free," 58–59

Bosco, P. J., 45, 49

Bostic, D., 40–41, 51

Boulware, D., 68, 76

Brannon, R., 19, 33, 92

Briggs, L. R., 80

Brown, R. W., 80, 88

C

Cambodian students, 36

Campus environment. *See* College environment

Canon, H. J., 19, 22, 34

Career choice: and child rearing issues, 26; and gender role strain, 26